Navigating Your Dream Job

Strategies for Success During a Recession

By

Gary Covella, Ph.D.

While every precaution has been taken in the preparation of this book, the publisher assumes no responsibility for errors or omissions, or for damages resulting from the use of the information contained herein.

NAVIGATING YOUR DREAM JOB: STRATEGIES FOR SUCCESS DURING A RECESSION

Contents

Navigating Your Dream Job

Chapter 1. Intro - Navigating Your Dream Job in a Competitive Market

Welcome to the first chapter of "Navigating Your Dream Job: Strategies for Success During a Recession". This book is your guide, your mentor, and your companion during uncertain economic times. It's designed to provide you with actionable strategies and insightful advice that will help you land your dream job, even when the economy seems to be against you.

Recessions can feel like an uphill battle, especially when it comes to job hunting. However, it's important to remember that challenges also present opportunities. While some industries may struggle, others thrive, and new career paths emerge. This book will help illuminate these possibilities and guide you toward them.

In this chapter, we'll start by understanding the current economic landscape. We'll explore what a recession means for job seekers, how it impacts different sectors, and how it changes the dynamics of the job market. We'll delve into real-time data from reliable sources such as the Bureau of Labor Statistics (www.bls.gov) and the World Economic Forum (www.weforum.org) to give you a comprehensive understanding of the situation.

Next, we'll discuss the mindset required to navigate a recession successfully. Times of economic downturn can be stressful and disheartening, but maintaining a positive and proactive attitude is key. We'll talk about resilience, adaptability, and the importance of lifelong learning in an ever-evolving job market.

Finally, we'll introduce you to the core strategies that will drive your job search during a recession. These strategies are not just about finding any job; they're about finding the right job. We'll discuss how to identify growth industries, how to leverage your transferable skills, and how to network effectively in a virtual world.

Throughout this journey, we'll hear from industry experts, recruitment specialists, and individuals who have successfully navigated their way to their dream jobs during previous recessions. Their stories and insights will inspire you, motivate you, and most importantly, show you that it is entirely possible to find your dream job during a recession.

So, let's get started. It's time to understand, strategize, and conquer your job search, no matter what the economy looks like. Welcome to the first step towards navigating your dream job during a recession.

Recognizing the Impact of Recession on Job Markets

Recessions are an inevitable part of economic cycles. They can be challenging times for many, especially those seeking employment or looking to change careers. Understanding the impact of a recession on job markets is crucial to effectively navigate your path toward your dream job during these uncertain times.

The Nature of Recessions and Job Markets

A recession is a period of significant decline in economic activity that lasts more than a few months. It's visible in real GDP, real income, employment, industrial production, and wholesale-retail sales. A common misconception is that a recession equates to fewer jobs across all sectors. While it's true that some sectors contract significantly during a downturn, others may remain stable or even grow.

For instance, during the Great Recession (2007-2009), industries like construction and manufacturing were severely impacted, resulting in substantial job losses. In contrast, sectors like healthcare and education experienced growth. Similarly, the COVID-19-induced recession saw a surge in demand for digital services, leading to growth in the tech sector amidst widespread economic turmoil.

Identifying Growth Sectors

Recognizing which sectors are likely to grow during a recession can help you better position yourself in the job market. Jobs in healthcare, education, and public safety often prove resilient during economic downturns. These sectors provide essential services that remain in demand, regardless of the economic climate.

In recent years, the technology sector has also demonstrated resilience during recessions. As businesses and consumers increasingly rely on digital services, tech companies continue to grow. For job seekers with relevant skills, this presents an opportunity to pivot towards these growing sectors.

The Rise of Remote Work

The impact of a recession on job markets isn't limited to shifts in sector growth. Changes in work patterns, such as the rise of remote work, also play a significant role. The COVID-19 pandemic has accelerated this trend, with companies across various sectors adopting remote work policies. This development has broadened the geographical scope of job opportunities, allowing job seekers to apply for positions beyond their immediate location.

Leveraging Transferable Skills

As the job market evolves during a recession, so too should your approach to finding your dream job. One effective strategy involves identifying and leveraging your transferable skills. These are abilities that are valuable across different jobs and sectors, such as communication, problem-solving, and leadership.

For example, if you've gained project management skills in a construction role but find opportunities in this sector limited during a recession, you could leverage these skills to transition into a project management role within a growing sector like technology or healthcare.

Recessions undeniably affect job markets, but they also present opportunities for those who can adapt. By understanding the nature of recessions and their impact on different sectors, identifying growth industries, embracing new work patterns, and leveraging your transferable skills, you can navigate your way toward your dream job, even during a downturn.

Remember, the key to success lies not in resisting change, but in adapting to it. The strategies outlined in this chapter will equip you with the knowledge and tools to do just that, enabling you to turn the challenge of a recession into an opportunity for career growth and progression.

Embracing the Challenge: Turning Adversity into Opportunity

In the face of a recession and its inevitable impact on job markets, it's easy to feel overwhelmed. The path to your dream job may seem more challenging than ever before. But remember, every adversity carries with it the seed of an equivalent or greater benefit. In this chapter, we'll explore how to turn the challenges of a recession into opportunities for career growth and advancement.

Adopting a Growth Mindset

The first step towards turning adversity into opportunity is adopting a growth mindset. This concept, coined by psychologist Carol Dweck, refers to the belief that abilities and intelligence can be developed through dedication and hard work. In the context of a job search during a recession, a growth mindset could mean viewing this challenging time as a chance to learn, grow, and adapt rather than as an insurmountable obstacle.

Upskilling and Reskilling

Recessions often accelerate trends that were already in motion, such as digitization and automation. This can lead to significant shifts in the skills that employers value. Upskilling (learning new skills to perform your current job) and reskilling (learning new skills for a different job) can be powerful tools for navigating these changes.

Online platforms like Coursera, edX, and LinkedIn Learning offer a plethora of courses across a wide range of industries, allowing you to upgrade your skills from the comfort of your home. By proactively upskilling or reskilling, you can position yourself as a valuable candidate in sectors that are growing during the recession.

Networking in a Digital World

Building a strong professional network is always important, but it becomes crucial during a recession when job openings may not be widely advertised. With many in-person networking events canceled due to social distancing measures, online networking has taken center stage.

LinkedIn is a powerful tool for connecting with professionals in your industry, attending virtual events, and staying updated on job opportunities. Other platforms like Twitter and industry-specific forums can also be valuable networking resources.

Creating Your Opportunities

If traditional job opportunities are scarce, consider creating your own. This could mean starting a freelance business, consulting, or even launching a start-up. Websites like Upwork and Fiverr can be great platforms to kickstart a freelancing career, while local business resources can guide starting your own business.

While a recession presents undeniable challenges, it also offers unique opportunities for those willing to embrace change. By adopting a growth mindset, upskilling or reskilling, leveraging digital networking, and creating your opportunities, you can turn the adversity of a recession into a stepping stone toward your dream job.

Remember, it's not the challenge that defines us, but how we respond to it. With resilience, adaptability, and determination, you can navigate the stormy seas of a recession and steer your career toward the safe harbor of your dream job.

The Importance of Strategy in a Competitive Market
In a recession, the job market becomes more competitive as the number of job seekers increases and the number of available positions decreases. This heightened competition makes it crucial to have a robust job search strategy. In this chapter, we'll delve into the importance of strategy in a competitive market and how you can craft your own to secure your dream job.

Understanding Job Market Dynamics

Before you can develop an effective strategy, it's vital to understand the dynamics of the job market during a recession. Some sectors may be hiring less, while others might be expanding their workforce. It's also important to note that many companies might be shifting their focus toward roles that can help them navigate through challenging times. By understanding these dynamics, you can tailor your strategy to align with the current needs of employers.

Crafting a Targeted Job Search

In a competitive market, a targeted job search is more effective than a broad, unfocused approach. This means identifying specific industries, companies, and roles that align with your skills, interests, and career goals. A targeted search allows you to focus your time and energy on opportunities where you have the highest chance of success.

Online job boards like Indeed and Glassdoor can be valuable resources for researching companies and roles.

LinkedIn can also provide insights into industry trends and allow you to connect directly with potential employers.

Building a Personal Brand

In a competitive job market, standing out from the crowd is crucial. One way to do this is by building a personal brand. This involves showcasing your unique skills, experiences, and perspectives in a way that positions you as a valuable asset to potential employers.

Your brand should be reflected in all aspects of your job search, from your resume and cover letter to your online presence. Websites like Canva can help you create visually appealing resumes, while platforms like LinkedIn and Medium allow you to share your thoughts and insights, further establishing your professional identity.

Emphasizing Adaptability and Resilience

During a recession, adaptability and resilience are highly valued traits. Companies are looking for employees who can navigate change, solve problems, and continue to perform under challenging circumstances. Highlighting examples of these traits in your previous roles can make you a more attractive candidate.

A recession may make the job market more competitive, but with a strong strategy, you can rise above the competition. By understanding market dynamics, crafting a targeted job search, building a personal brand, and emphasizing your adaptability and resilience, you can increase your chances of landing your dream job, even in a challenging economic climate.

Remember, a strategy is not a one-size-fits-all solution but a personalized plan that plays to your strengths and aligns with your career goals. With the right strategy, you can turn the challenge of a recession into an opportunity for career growth and advancement.

Identifying Your Unique Selling Proposition

In the quest for your dream job during a recession, one of the most crucial elements to consider is your unique selling proposition (USP). Your USP is what sets you apart from other candidates in the job market. It's a combination of skills, experiences, and personal traits that make you uniquely suited to a particular role or industry. In this chapter, we'll explore how to identify your USP and leverage it to stand out in a competitive job market.

Understanding the Concept of a Unique Selling Proposition The concept of a USP originates from the world of marketing, where it's used to differentiate a product or service from its competitors. When applied to job hunting, your USP becomes the unique mix of qualities that make you the best fit for a role.

Your USP could include hard skills related to your profession, soft skills like communication or leadership, specific experiences you've had, or even personal characteristics that align with a company's culture. The key is to identify what makes you unique and how those qualities bring value to potential employers.

Reflecting on Your Skills and Experiences

To identify your USP, start by reflecting on your skills and experiences. Consider the roles you've excelled in, the projects you've completed, and the skills you've developed along the way. Think about the feedback you've received from colleagues or supervisors - what strengths do they consistently highlight?

Online tools like SkillScan or CliftonStrengths can help you identify and articulate your skills and strengths. These insights can form the foundation of your USP.

Aligning with Employer Needs

Your USP should not only reflect your strengths but also align with what employers are looking for. Research your target industry and roles to understand the skills and qualities that are in demand. Job descriptions on platforms like LinkedIn or Indeed can provide valuable insights into what employers value.

Communicating Your USP

Once you've identified your USP, it's essential to communicate it effectively. This should be reflected in every aspect of your job search - your resume, cover letter, online profiles, and interviews. Each interaction with potential employers is an opportunity to reinforce your USP.

Websites like Canva can help you design a resume that highlights your unique qualities, while a platform like

LinkedIn allows you to showcase your USP to a broad professional audience.

Identifying your unique selling proposition is a powerful step toward securing your dream job during a recession. By understanding what sets you apart and aligning this with employer needs, you can position yourself as a standout candidate in a competitive job market.

Remember, your USP is not just about what you can do, but who you are. Embrace your uniqueness and let it shine through in your job search. After all, there's only one you, and that's your greatest advantage.

Deciphering Economic Indicators and Their Impact on Jobs In our journey through "Navigating Your Dream Job: Strategies for Success During a Recession," we've arrived at a crucial chapter. Understanding economic indicators is like learning to read the road signs of your job search adventure. These indicators can tell us about the health of the economy, which sectors are growing, and where job opportunities might be found.

Understanding Economic Indicators

Economic indicators are statistics that provide insights into the overall health of an economy. They can be leading (predictive), coincident (contemporary), or lagging (historical). Leading indicators, such as stock market performance and building permits issued, offer a glimpse into the future economic situation. Coincident indicators, like GDP and retail sales data, reflect the current state of the economy. Lagging indicators, such as unemployment rates and corporate profits, provide information about past economic performance.

For example, the U.S. Bureau of Labor Statistics (www.bls.gov) provides comprehensive data on employment, unemployment, and pay & benefits across various sectors. Similarly, the U.S. Department of Commerce's Bureau of Economic Analysis (www.bea.gov) offers detailed accounts of U.S. economic accounts, including GDP and personal income and outlays data.

Economic Indicators and Job Markets

The relationship between economic indicators and the job market is intricate. A healthy economy typically signifies a robust job market, but the correlation isn't always direct. For instance, even in a booming economy, technological advancements can lead to job losses in certain sectors. Conversely, during a recession, some sectors may still experience growth and job creation.

An excellent example of this is the 'Great Recession' of 2008. While many sectors faced significant job losses, others like healthcare and education continued to grow. The key is to understand which sectors are likely to expand or contract based on economic indicators.

Leveraging Economic Indicators in Your Job Search

Economic indicators can guide your job search in several ways. If the indicators suggest a strong economy, it might be a good time to consider changing jobs or negotiating a higher salary. In a weaker economy, you might want to focus on sectors that traditionally do well during recessions, like healthcare or utilities.

Additionally, regional economic indicators can help you decide where to focus your job search. For instance, if a particular region is experiencing significant economic growth, it could be an excellent place to look for job opportunities.

In conclusion, understanding economic indicators and their impact on jobs is a critical skill for navigating the job market during a recession. By staying informed and making strategic decisions based on these indicators, you can improve your chances of landing your dream job, even in challenging economic times.

In the next chapter, we will delve deeper into how to adapt your job search strategy based on the economic climate and explore how to position yourself effectively in a competitive job market. Stay tuned!

Industry Analysis: Who's Hiring, Who's Firing

As we navigate the challenging terrain of a recession, it becomes crucial to identify those industries that stand firm, continuing to hire amidst the economic upheaval. Here are some sectors where you might find your dream job:

Education Services: Even in the face of economic downturns, the demand for education services remains steadfast. For current opportunities in this sector, consider visiting education job boards such as EdJoin at www.edjoin.org or SchoolSpring at www.schoolspring.com.

Healthcare: The consistent need for healthcare professionals makes this sector largely immune to recessions. Websites like HealthcareJobsite at www.healthcarejobsite.com and Health eCareers at www.healthecareers.com can provide a plethora of opportunities.

Federal Government: The stability of federal government careers makes them a safe harbor in turbulent economic times. Check out USAJobs at www.usajobs.gov for a comprehensive list of available positions.

Public Utilities: Public utilities, being essential services, maintain a steady demand for employees. Websites such as PublicServiceCareers at www.publicservicecareers.org can be a valuable resource for job seekers.

Law Enforcement: The persistent need for law enforcement officers makes this field a reliable choice. Visit pages like LawEnforcementJob at www.lawenforcementjob.com for potential opportunities.

Specialized Care, Therapy, and Counseling: These professions are always in demand, indicating promising hiring prospects. Websites like TherapyJobs at www.therapyjobs.com offer a range of job listings in this sector.

Financial Services: Interestingly, this sector often flourishes even in the face of a recession. Job seekers can explore opportunities on sites like eFinancialCareers at www.efinancialcareers.com.

While these sectors are generally considered recession-proof, it's important to remember that the hiring situation can vary based on factors such as location and the severity of the recession. Therefore, for the most accurate information, it's best to visit the websites of companies within these industries directly. In the next chapter, we will explore how to make your applications and interviews stand out in these resilient sectors.

The Role of Technology and Digitalization During a Recession

Recessions are testing times for businesses, bringing about economic uncertainty that can challenge even the most resilient enterprises. However, amidst these trials, technology and digitalization have emerged as pivotal tools that can help businesses navigate the turbulent waters of an economic downturn.

Technology as a Catalyst

Investing in technology during a recession can enable businesses to surge ahead when the market rebounds. The key lies in focusing on efficiency, productivity, customer relationships, communication, and sales volume. By leveraging technology, companies can optimize their spending while still delivering strong customer value and a memorable customer experience.

For instance, new technologies like cloud migrations, Artificial Intelligence (AI), and automation can drive cost reductions. Enhancements of current products or services through digital technologies can also provide a competitive edge.

Digital Transformation: A Necessity, Not a Luxury
In times of economic crises, digital transformation initiatives become more than just large line items in tech leaders' budgets—they become a lifeline. An offensive digital strategy, prioritizing digital investments, securing talent, and finding cost-efficiencies through digital means become essential strategies for survival and growth.

Digital transformation is not just relevant during a recession—it's crucial. Businesses need to leverage the digital solutions they already have in place and invest in new ones that will meet the evolving demands of their customers.

The Unequal Embrace of Digitalization

While digitalization has immense potential to ease the effects of a recession, it's important to note the inequalities that might arise from an unequal embrace of digitalization. There is mounting evidence that these inequalities could contribute to the macroeconomic conditions marked by high recession risks. Therefore, businesses and policymakers alike must ensure that digital opportunities are accessible to all.

Digital Occupations: A Silver Lining

The recent COVID-19 recession led to an increase in demand for digital occupations in the United States. This trend highlights the resilience of the tech industry during economic downturns. While no job is entirely recession-proof, certain roles within the tech field have shown consistent demand and stability, making them attractive career paths even during times of economic uncertainty.

Digitally leading companies are more likely to make additional technology investments during a recession, which can set them up for success in the long run. As we move forward in an increasingly digital era, the role of technology and digitalization during a recession will only become more prominent. Leveraging these tools effectively can be the difference between merely surviving a recession and emerging from it stronger than ever.

Understanding the Shift in Employer Expectations

In the wake of a recession, the job market transforms drastically. One significant change is the shift in employer expectations. As businesses grapple with economic uncertainty, they redefine what they expect from their employees. Understanding this shift is crucial for anyone hoping to secure their dream job during a recession.

Emphasis on Adaptability

In an uncertain economy, adaptability becomes a highly sought-after trait. Employers want employees who can adjust to changing circumstances and continue to deliver results. This means being open to new ways of doing things, learning new skills, and taking on different roles as needed. Demonstrating a willingness to adapt and grow can make you stand out to potential employers.

Mastery of Digital Tools

As businesses increasingly turn to digital solutions to weather the storm of a recession, proficiency in digital tools becomes more important than ever. From communication platforms like Slack and Microsoft Teams to project management tools like Trello or Asana, mastering these digital tools can significantly increase your employability.

Strong Communication Skills

With remote work becoming more common, strong communication skills have become even more essential. Employers are looking for candidates who can express their ideas clearly and effectively, whether it's through email, video conferencing, or instant messaging. Being able to articulate your thoughts and understand others' perspectives is crucial in a virtual work environment.

A Focus on Results

When times are tough, employers need employees who can deliver results. This means demonstrating not just your skills and knowledge, but also your ability to use those assets to achieve tangible outcomes. When applying for jobs or going for interviews, focus on the results you've achieved in past roles and how you can bring that same level of success to your potential employer.

Emotional Intelligence

Emotional intelligence, or the ability to understand and manage your own emotions and those of others, is another quality that employers value highly, especially during challenging times. Employees with high emotional intelligence can navigate difficult situations with empathy and resilience, making them invaluable assets to their teams.

Recessions can be challenging, but they also provide opportunities to learn, grow, and adapt. By understanding how employer expectations shift during these times, you can better position yourself to secure your dream job. Remember, it's not just about having the right skills—it's also about demonstrating the right mindset. With adaptability, digital proficiency, strong communication skills, a results-oriented approach, and emotional intelligence, you can show potential employers that you're exactly the kind of employee they need to navigate a recession successfully.

The Influence of Global Trends on Local Job Markets

In the interconnected world that we live in, global trends significantly influence local job markets. These trends shape the demand for different skills, the types of jobs available, and where these jobs are located. Consequently, understanding these trends is crucial for anyone looking to navigate their career path during a recession.

The Rise of Remote Work

One of the most significant trends reshaping job markets worldwide is the rise of remote work. The COVID-19 pandemic has accelerated this shift, with many companies now offering flexible work arrangements. This change has broadened the geographical scope of job opportunities, enabling people to work for companies based in different cities or even countries. Websites like Remote.co (https://remote.co/) and FlexJobs (https://www.flexjobs.com/) can be excellent resources for finding remote work opportunities.

Automation and Artificial Intelligence

Another major trend influencing job markets is the rise of automation and artificial intelligence (AI). While these technologies may reduce demand for certain jobs, especially those involving repetitive tasks, they also create new opportunities in fields like AI, machine learning, and data analysis. Websites like Kaggle (https://www.kaggle.com/) and Coursera (https://www.coursera.org/) offer resources and courses for those interested in these growing fields.

Transition to a Green Economy

As the world grapples with climate change, there's a growing push towards a green economy. This shift is creating new jobs in areas such as renewable energy, sustainable agriculture, and green construction. Websites like GreenJobs (https://www.greenjobs.com/) offer specialized job boards for those seeking employment in these industries.

Emphasis on Upskilling and Reskilling

The rapid pace of technological change is shortening the lifecycle of many skills, leading to a growing emphasis on lifelong learning. Employers are increasingly looking for workers who can adapt and learn new skills. Websites like LinkedIn Learning (https://www.linkedin.com/learning/) and Udemy (https://www.udemy.com/) provide a wealth of online courses for upskilling and reskilling.

Expansion of the Gig Economy

The gig economy continues to grow, providing more flexible, project-based work opportunities. This trend is changing the job market by offering alternative paths to traditional full-time employment. Websites like Upwork (https://www.upwork.com/) and Freelancer (https://www.freelancer.com/) connect freelancers with businesses seeking their skills.

Global trends play a significant role in shaping local job markets. By keeping an eye on these trends and adapting accordingly, job seekers can better position themselves to find their dream job, even during a recession. Remember, in a rapidly changing job market, flexibility, adaptability, and a willingness to learn new skills are key to success.

Chapter 2: Understanding the Current Job Market

The job market can be a daunting place, especially during times of economic uncertainty. With global trends changing the way employers view candidates and technology reshaping traditional roles, it's more important than ever to understand the current job market before beginning your search. In this chapter, we'll explore how AI tools like ChatGPT are transforming the recruitment process and discuss strategies for navigating this challenging landscape with confidence. We'll look at ways to assess your skillset and develop a growth mindset while building professional networks and crafting an effective personal brand. Finally, we'll bring together all of these key points in a concise manner to provide insight into how you can gain a competitive edge in today's job market.

The State of the Global Economy

Understanding the global economy's state is a crucial step in successfully navigating your dream job during a recession. This chapter will provide an overview of the current economic landscape and its implications on employment.

The global economy has seen significant turbulence in recent years. Trade conflicts, geopolitical tensions, and most notably, the COVID-19 pandemic have left lasting impacts. According to the World Economic Outlook report by the International Monetary Fund (IMF), the global economy contracted by 3.5% in 2020. More insights can be found at www.imf.org/en/Publications/WEO/Issues/2021/01/26/2021-world-economic-outlook-update

However, it's not all doom and gloom. The same IMF report predicts a robust recovery in 2021, with global growth expected to reach 6%. This hopeful forecast comes on the heels of unprecedented financial support from governments worldwide and the successful rollout of vaccines, which are expected to control the pandemic's spread and stimulate economic recovery.

However, it's important to note that this recovery won't be uniform across all sectors or regions. Some industries, such as technology and e-commerce, have flourished during the pandemic, while others, like hospitality and tourism, face a more challenging recovery path.

For example, the technology sector has seen an explosion in demand due to the shift towards remote work and online learning. Companies like Zoom and Slack have become indispensable tools for many, and this trend toward digital transformation is expected to continue even after the pandemic subsides.

Conversely, the hospitality and tourism sectors have been hit hard, with travel restrictions leading to a dramatic drop in international tourism. According to the United Nations World Tourism Organization (UNWTO), international tourist arrivals fell by 74% in 2020. For more information, visit www.unwto.org/news/international-tourism-back-to-1990-levels-as-arrivals-fall-by-more-than-70.

These industry trends can help guide your career choices. If you're interested in a career in technology, now might be an opportune time to refine your skills and seize opportunities. If you're in a struggling sector like tourism, it might be worth considering a transition to a more resilient industry.

Regional trends also play a significant role. While some economies, such as China and Vietnam, have managed to maintain positive growth rates in 2020, many Western economies have seen substantial contractions. Understanding these regional differences can shape your job search strategy and open up new opportunities.

The global economy is in a state of flux, presenting both challenges and opportunities. By staying informed and adaptable, you can navigate these uncertain times and move closer towards securing your dream job. In the following chapter, we'll explore strategies for job hunting during a recession, leveraging our understanding of the current economic landscape.

Trends in Job Availability

In the rapidly evolving world of work, staying abreast of trends in job availability is key to successfully navigating your career during a recession. This chapter aims to explore some of the major trends that are shaping the job market.

One of the most significant shifts we've seen recently is the move towards remote work. Triggered by the COVID-19 pandemic, this trend has transformed the traditional office environment and is expected to persist. More companies are adopting hybrid models where employees can enjoy the flexibility of splitting their time between the office and home.

The technology sector, particularly areas such as artificial intelligence, machine learning, and data science, continues its upward trajectory. As digital transformation accelerates across all sectors, the demand for tech-savvy professionals is on the rise.

Simultaneously, the world's focus on climate change is leading to an increase in green jobs. Roles in renewable energy, sustainability, and environmental science are gaining prominence as we collectively strive for a more sustainable future.

The health sector is another area where job growth is anticipated. Driven by an aging population and ongoing public health challenges, healthcare professionals' demand is expected to remain robust.

Another trend to keep an eye on is the growth of the gig economy. Freelance and contract work are becoming more mainstream as individuals seek flexible working arrangements. This shift is changing the employment landscape, offering both opportunities and challenges for job seekers.

Finally, as the pace of technological change accelerates, upskilling and reskilling are becoming increasingly important. The ability to continuously learn and adapt to new tools and technologies is becoming a crucial skill in the modern workplace.

Industries on the Rise

Navigating your dream job during a recession involves understanding which sectors are resilient and growing, despite economic downturns. This chapter will explore several industries that have historically shown such resilience.

The healthcare industry often proves to be recession-resistant. Regardless of economic conditions, there is a constant demand for health services, making this sector a stable choice. From frontline healthcare providers to health tech innovators, a vast array of roles can offer a rewarding career in this industry.

Information technology is another sector that tends to thrive, even in challenging economic times. The shift towards digital transformation, accelerated by the adoption of remote work, has led to an increased demand for IT services. Whether you're a software developer, data analyst, or IT project manager, there's a strong likelihood of finding robust job opportunities in this field.

E-commerce has seen a significant surge in recent years, spurred by changing consumer behaviors. As more people embrace online shopping, particularly in the wake of the COVID-19 pandemic, online retail has emerged as a resilient and growing industry. Roles in this sector can range from digital marketing to logistics and supply chain management.

Grocery retail is another industry that tends to hold steady during recessions. People continue to buy food and other essentials, regardless of the economy's state. Thus, careers in grocery retail, from store management to procurement, can offer stability.

Lastly, the education and training sector often sees a rise during economic downturns. Job loss can lead to an increased need for retraining and upskilling, driving demand for educational services. This trend opens up opportunities for educators, course developers, and e-learning specialists.

Impact of Remote Work

The advent of remote work has undeniably reshaped the global job market. This new trend, accelerated by the

COVID-19 pandemic, has left an indelible mark on how we conduct business and navigate our careers.

Remote work has democratized the job market in many ways. It has broken down geographical barriers that previously limited job opportunities. Now, a company headquartered in San Francisco can seamlessly employ someone living in a small town hundreds of miles away, or even in another country. This broadens the scope for job seekers, opening up a world of opportunities that were previously out of reach.

This shift has also led to a greater emphasis on work-life balance. Without the daily commute and with more control over their schedule, many workers find they have more time for personal pursuits and family commitments. Companies are recognizing this and are increasingly promoting flexible working conditions as part of their employee value proposition.

However, the rise of remote work isn't without its challenges. The blurring of boundaries between work and home life can lead to burnout. Workers may feel they're "always on" and struggle to switch off from work. Therefore, it's crucial to establish clear boundaries and take regular breaks to maintain mental well-being.

Additionally, remote work requires a specific set of skills. Self-discipline, strong communication, and familiarity with digital tools are all key to succeeding in a remote role. If you're seeking a remote job, it's worth investing time in developing these skills.

The shift to remote work also impacts the types of jobs that are in demand. Roles that can be performed digitally, such as in tech, digital marketing, and customer support, have seen an increase in demand. Conversely, jobs requiring physical presence or face-to-face interaction may have seen a decline.

It's also worth noting that remote work has environmental implications. With fewer people commuting daily, carbon emissions can be significantly reduced. For those passionate about sustainability, remote work aligns with these values.

The rise of remote work is a game-changer for job seekers. It presents both exciting opportunities and unique challenges. By understanding its impact, you can better position yourself to navigate your dream job during a recession.

Predictions for the Future

Predicting the future is a challenging endeavor, particularly in the complex and ever-changing realm of employment and economics. However, by observing current trends and patterns, we can make some educated guesses about what the future might hold. In this chapter, we'll explore some predictions that could shape your job search strategy during a recession.

Perhaps the most significant trend shaping the future of work is digital transformation. The adoption of digital technologies across industries has accelerated due to the pandemic, changing how companies operate and compete. This transformation is expected to continue, leading to greater demand for roles in technology, data analysis, and digital marketing.

Another significant trend is the shift towards more flexible work arrangements. The rise of remote work has shown both employers and employees that productivity can be maintained outside traditional office environments. As such, flexible and remote working options will likely become more commonplace in the future.

Moreover, the growing awareness of climate change and sustainability is likely to shape the job market. Green jobs in sectors like renewable energy, sustainability consulting, and conservation are expected to increase as companies strive to reduce their environmental impact.

Furthermore, the ongoing advancements in artificial intelligence and automation will undoubtedly impact the job market. While these technologies might displace certain jobs, they will also create new ones. Roles that involve the development, management, and ethical oversight of these technologies are likely to be in high demand.

Lastly, the gig economy is likely to continue growing. The trend towards freelance and contract work provides flexibility for workers and allows companies to tap into a global talent pool.

To stay informed about the latest developments and trends, consider regularly checking reliable sources such as the Bureau of Labor Statistics (www.bls.gov) and the World Economic Forum (www.weforum.org).

While the future is inherently uncertain, being aware of these potential trends can help you prepare and adapt. By staying informed and flexible, you can navigate the challenges of a recession and move closer to securing your dream job.

Chapter 3: Identifying Your Dream Job

Amid an economic recession, it's easy to feel lost and uncertain about your professional future. However, with the right mindset and a strategic approach, you can navigate through these challenging times and secure your dream job. The first crucial step is self-assessment and setting clear career goals.

Understanding Self-Assessment

Self-assessment is the process of evaluating your skills, interests, values, personality traits, and passions. It's all about taking an introspective look at what you're good at, what you enjoy doing, and what truly matters to you in a job.

Many online platforms offer self-assessment tests. For instance, Myers-Briggs Type Indicator and The Big Five Personality Test are two popular personality assessments that can offer valuable insights into your work style and preferences.

Similarly, O*NET Interest Profiler is a free online tool that can help you discover what your work-related interests are and how they relate to various jobs.

Setting Career Goals

Once you've gained a deeper understanding of yourself, it's time to set your career goals. Career goals are targets that guide your career path and motivate you to achieve more. They provide a sense of direction and help you focus your efforts on what's important.

When setting career goals, consider both short-term and long-term objectives. Short-term goals typically span a few months to a couple of years, while long-term goals may take several years or even decades to achieve.

For instance, a short-term goal could be to gain a specific certification or skill, while a long-term goal might be to become a department head or start your own business.

Remember to make your goals SMART - Specific, Measurable, Achievable, Relevant, and Time-bound. MindTools offers an excellent guide on how to set SMART goals.

Aligning Self-Assessment and Career Goals

Now that you've assessed yourself and set your career goals, it's time to align the two. This involves identifying the skills, knowledge, and experiences you need to achieve your career goals based on your self-assessment.

For example, if your self-assessment reveals that you have a knack for problem-solving and your career goal is to become a project manager, you might need to pursue further training in project management methodologies.

Self-assessment and setting career goals are vital steps in finding your dream job during a recession. By knowing who you are and what you want, you will be better equipped to seize opportunities and overcome obstacles on your career journey. Remember, every challenge presents an opportunity for growth and learning. So, embrace this journey with an open mind and a determined spirit.

Researching Job Profiles

In the journey of finding your dream job during an economic recession, understanding job profiles is a critical step. By researching job profiles, you can gain insights into the roles and responsibilities, skills required, salary expectations, and career progression paths of various jobs. This knowledge can guide you in choosing the right career path and preparing effectively for it.

Understanding Job Profiles

A job profile outlines the key aspects of a particular job. It includes the job title, primary duties, required skills and qualifications, work environment, and compensation details.

You can find job profiles on various online platforms. Websites like LinkedIn and Indeed provide comprehensive job descriptions posted by employers. Another valuable resource is the Bureau of Labor Statistics' Occupational Outlook Handbook, which provides in-depth information about hundreds of occupations.

Evaluating Job Profiles

When evaluating job profiles, consider aspects like job duties, required skills, qualifications, work-life balance, salary, and prospects.

For instance, if you're interested in a career in digital marketing, look for job profiles such as 'Digital Marketing Specialist', 'SEO Manager', or 'Content Strategist'. Evaluate each profile based on your interests, skills, and career goals.

Matching Job Profiles with Your Career Goals

After evaluating various job profiles, try to match them with your career goals. If a job profile aligns with your short-term and long-term goals, it could be a good fit for you.

For example, if one of your career goals is to work in a leadership role, look for job profiles that offer opportunities for growth and advancement.

Networking and Informational Interviews

Networking and informational interviews can also provide valuable insights into different job profiles. Reach out to professionals in your fields of interest through LinkedIn or professional networking events. Ask them about their job, the skills they use, their career path, and any advice they have for someone interested in their field.

Researching job profiles is a crucial step in finding your dream job during a recession. It helps you understand what employers are looking for and how you can prepare effectively. Remember, knowledge is power. The more you know about the job market and specific job profiles, the better equipped you will be to navigate your career path successfully.

Aligning Passion with Profession

In the quest for your dream job, particularly during a recession, aligning your passion with your profession is a powerful strategy. It's about finding a career that not only pays the bills but also fulfills you and makes you look forward to each workday.

The Power of Passion

Passion is a strong inclination towards an activity that you find enjoyable and in which you invest time and energy. When your profession aligns with your passion, work becomes more than just a means to an end. It becomes a source of fulfillment and purpose.

According to a study by Deloitte, passionate workers are more likely to be committed to their jobs, resilient in the face of challenges, and willing to go the extra mile.

Identifying Your Passion

Identifying your passion begins with introspection. Reflect on activities that you love doing, topics that you're naturally curious about, and issues that you care deeply about.

Various online tools can help you identify your passions. Websites like 16Personalities and VIA Character Strengths Survey can provide insights into your personality traits and strengths, which can guide you toward your passions.

Turning Passion into a Profession

Once you've identified your passion, the next step is to determine how it can translate into a viable profession.

For instance, if you're passionate about writing, professions that might align with your passion include copywriting, journalism, content marketing, or even authorship.

Research these professions using platforms like LinkedIn, Indeed, and the Bureau of Labor Statistics' Occupational Outlook Handbook. Understand the skills required, the typical career path, and the market demand for these roles.

Balancing Passion with Practicality

While it's important to follow your passion, it's equally vital to balance it with practicality. Consider factors like job market trends, salary expectations, and job security.

For example, you might be passionate about a field with limited job opportunities. In such cases, consider related fields or roles where you could apply your passion.

Alternatively, you could pursue your passion as a side project or hobby while working in a more stable job.

Aligning your passion with your profession can be a game-changer in your pursuit of the dream job, especially during a recession. It can lead to higher job satisfaction, better performance, and a greater sense of fulfillment. Remember, your dream job lies at the intersection of what you love, what you're good at, and what the world needs. So, dare to follow your passion and make it your profession.

Evaluating Company Culture

As you navigate the path to your dream job during a recession, understanding and evaluating a company's culture is a key factor to consider. A company's culture can significantly impact your job satisfaction, work-life balance, and overall career growth.

The Importance of Company Culture

Company culture refers to the shared values, behaviors, and beliefs that characterize an organization. It includes aspects like leadership style, communication patterns, employee relations, work environment, and company mission. It's the 'personality' of the company and shapes how work gets done.

A positive company culture can foster creativity, productivity, and employee engagement. On the other hand, negative or mismatched company culture can lead to stress, low morale, and high turnover rates.

Researching Company Culture

One way to evaluate a company's culture is by researching online. Websites like Glassdoor and LinkedIn provide valuable insights into companies from employees' perspectives. You can read reviews, observe company updates, and see how the company presents itself to the world.

The company's website can also offer clues about its culture. Look at their mission, vision, and values, and see if they align with yours. Pay attention to the language they use, the images they choose, and any information about their work environment or employee benefits.

Observing the Work Environment

If you get the chance to visit the company premises for an interview, observe the work environment. Look at the office layout, the interactions between employees, the dress code, and even the small details like cleanliness and decor. These can all provide hints about the company culture.

Asking Questions

During job interviews, don't hesitate to ask questions about the company culture. You might ask about team collaboration, leadership style, work-life balance, diversity and inclusion efforts, or how the company handles feedback and criticism.

Reflecting on Your Preferences

Finally, reflect on what kind of culture you thrive in. Do you prefer a formal, structured environment or a casual, flexible one? Do you value teamwork and collaboration, or do you work best independently? Understanding your preferences can help you evaluate whether a company's culture is a good fit for you.

Evaluating a company's culture is a critical step in finding your dream job during a recession. It can affect not just your job satisfaction, but also your mental well-being and career growth. So, take the time to research, observe, ask questions, and reflect on what kind of culture suits you best. Remember, a job is not just about the paycheck; it's also about finding a place where you can grow and thrive.

The Role of Salary and Benefits

In the pursuit of your dream job during a recession, salary and benefits play a significant role. While passion and job satisfaction are important, financial compensation and additional perks can greatly impact your quality of life and job satisfaction.

Understanding Salary Expectations

Salary is a crucial factor to consider when job hunting. It's not just about meeting your basic needs; it's also about being fairly compensated for your skills, experience, and contributions to the company.

Websites like Glassdoor, Payscale, and Salary.com can help you understand the average salary range for specific roles in different industries and locations. This information can guide you in setting realistic salary expectations and negotiating your pay effectively.

Considering Employee Benefits

In addition to salary, employee benefits are an integral part of your compensation package. They include aspects like health insurance, retirement plans, paid time off, flexible working hours, professional development opportunities, and more.

According to a survey by Aflac, 60% of employees are likely to accept a job with lower pay if it offered better benefits. This highlights the importance of considering benefits in your job search.

Balancing Salary and Benefits

While both salary and benefits are important, their relative significance might vary depending on your circumstances and priorities.

For example, if you have significant financial obligations, a high salary might be more important to you. On the other hand, if you value work-life balance or have specific healthcare needs, comprehensive benefits might hold more weight.

Negotiating Your Compensation

Once you've evaluated the salary and benefits for a job, don't hesitate to negotiate if you feel the offer doesn't meet your expectations or industry standards. Remember, negotiation is a normal part of the hiring process, and most employers expect it.

Websites like The Muse

(https://www.themuse.com/advice/how-to-negotiate-salary-37-tips-you-need-to-know) offer valuable tips on how to negotiate your salary and benefits effectively.

While finding your dream job during a recession may require some flexibility, understanding and evaluating the role of salary and benefits is crucial. It's about finding a balance between financial security, job satisfaction, and personal well-being. So, take the time to research, reflect on your needs and priorities, and don't be afraid to advocate for yourself. Remember, your skills and contributions are valuable, and you deserve to be compensated fairly for them.

Chapter 4: Preparing for Success with AI and ChatGPT

In the current job market, job seekers must stay ahead of the competition by using the latest tools and technologies. Artificial intelligence (AI) and ChatGPT are two such cutting-edge tools that can help you gain a competitive edge in your search for work. AI provides powerful insights into potential employers, while ChatGPT is an interactive chatbot platform providing personalized advice to job seekers. In this chapter, we discuss how to use these innovative solutions to prepare for success in today's challenging job market.

The AI Revolution: How It's Transforming the Job Market

In our modern world, the influence of Artificial Intelligence (AI) on the job market is profound and continues to evolve. This chapter will delve into this transformative technology's role in shaping employment trends and opportunities, especially during economic downturns.

AI is revolutionizing the way we work by automating repetitive tasks across a broad spectrum of industries. This shift is not merely about replacing human workers with machines; it's about transforming the nature of work itself. While AI might render certain jobs obsolete, it simultaneously paves the way for roles that require uniquely human attributes like creativity and problem-solving.

Reports from reputable sources such as the World Economic Forum highlight the dual-edged nature of AI's impact on employment. Their "The Future of Jobs Report 2020" suggests that while AI could replace up to 85% of jobs in specific sectors, it's also predicted to usher in new job roles that we can't even imagine today.

Goldman Sachs, a global leader in finance, has voiced similar concerns. They recently reported that generative AI technologies could potentially disrupt 300 million jobs worldwide. Interestingly, the jobs most at risk are those traditionally considered safe from automation, such as administrative and legal professions.

Yet, it's not all doom and gloom. AI is carving out its niche in recruitment, proving to be an invaluable tool for companies worldwide. Algorithms trained on vast datasets can delineate a company's ideal candidate profile, streamlining the hiring process by tracking and rating resumes submitted by prospective employees.

However, there's a gap between the public's perception of AI's impact and their readiness to adapt. A recent survey revealed that while 62 percent of Americans anticipate that

AI will significantly alter work and jobs over the next two decades, a mere 28 percent feel adequately prepared to navigate this change.

Despite potential disruptions, many experts remain optimistic about AI's overall net impact on job creation. Even amidst significant labor market churn, half of the organizations surveyed anticipate that AI will lead to job growth.

It's important to remember that the influence of AI on the job market is a rapidly evolving field. These points offer a snapshot of the current situation, providing a foundation to prepare for future changes. As the AI revolution marches on, staying informed and adaptable will be key to navigating your dream job successfully, even in times of recession.

Harnessing the Power of ChatGPT for Career Growth

In an era where technology and artificial intelligence (AI) are reshaping every facet of our lives, career advancement strategies must evolve to keep pace. One such AI innovation that's making waves is OpenAI's ChatGPT. This chapter will delve into how you can leverage this AI model for your career growth, even in times of recession.

ChatGPT is a language model developed by OpenAI, designed to generate human-like text based on the input it receives. It's been trained on a diverse range of internet text, enabling it to predict and generate responses that align with the context.

So, how can this remarkable piece of technology aid your career advancement? Let's explore some potential applications.

Firstly, ChatGPT can be an excellent tool for improving your communication skills. Whether drafting emails, writing reports, or crafting presentations, using an AI assistant like ChatGPT can help refine your language, ensuring that your written communication is clear, concise, and impactful.

Secondly, ChatGPT can be utilized as a learning tool. You can engage with it to learn about new topics, gain insights into complex subjects, or simply to stay updated with industry trends. Given its training on a wide array of internet text, ChatGPT can provide valuable information and perspectives on a multitude of subjects.

Thirdly, ChatGPT can serve as a virtual mentor, providing guidance and advice on various career-related matters. From brainstorming ideas for a project to discussing potential solutions for a workplace issue, ChatGPT can offer valuable insights that could propel your career forward.

Lastly, with more companies integrating AI into their operations, having firsthand experience with such technologies can give you a competitive edge. Familiarity with AI, especially models like ChatGPT, could make you a more attractive candidate to potential employers.

However, while the potential benefits of ChatGPT are immense, it's important to approach it with a critical mindset. Always cross-verify the information provided by the AI and remember that it doesn't replace human judgment or expertise.

ChatGPT is a powerful tool that can be harnessed for career advancement. By using it to enhance your communication skills, expand your knowledge, seek guidance, and gain exposure to AI, you can navigate your way toward your dream job, even during a recession.

Embracing AI in Your Job Search

As the digital revolution unfolds, Artificial Intelligence (AI) has emerged as a game-changer in various sectors, including job search. This chapter will delve into the ways you can leverage AI to streamline your job search process and land your dream job even during a recession.

To begin with, AI has significantly influenced the recruitment process with the advent of application tracking systems (ATS). These systems use AI algorithms to scan resumes and evaluate them based on keywords, work experience, and education. Understanding how these systems work can help you tailor your resume to increase your chances of being shortlisted. For instance, using relevant keywords and mirroring the language used in the job description can make your resume more ATS-friendly.

Next, AI-powered job search platforms have simplified the process of job hunting. Platforms like LinkedIn, Indeed, and Glassdoor use AI to match candidates with suitable job postings based on their skills, interests, and search history. By accurately filling out your profile and consistently engaging with these platforms, you can ensure that you're presented with job opportunities that align with your career goals.

AI is also making its mark in interview preparation. Tools like Interviewing.io and Pramp use AI to simulate real job interviews, providing valuable feedback and helping users improve their interview skills. These platforms can be particularly useful if you're transitioning into new roles or industries, as they allow you to practice and prepare for different types of interview questions.

Moreover, AI can help you stay updated with the latest industry trends and skills in demand. Platforms like Coursera and Udemy use AI to recommend courses based on your career interests and skill gaps. This can help you upskill and remain competitive in the job market, especially during a recession.

Lastly, AI chatbots have become increasingly popular in providing career advice. Platforms like Wade & Wendy and Mya employ AI chatbots to provide personalized job recommendations and career advice, making the job search process less daunting.

However, while AI can significantly aid your job search, it's important to remember that it should complement, not replace, traditional job search strategies. Networking, gaining relevant experience, and demonstrating soft skills are still crucial components of a successful job hunt.

Embracing AI can enhance your job search by making it more efficient and targeted. By understanding and leveraging AI, you can navigate the complexities of the job market and move closer to securing your dream job, even during challenging economic times.

Decoding AI in Recruitment

In today's technology-driven world, Artificial Intelligence (AI) has made its mark in the field of recruitment, revolutionizing the way talent acquisition is conducted. This chapter will delve into understanding AI's role in recruitment and how it can influence your job-seeking journey, especially during a recession.

AI in recruitment refers to the use of AI technologies, such as machine learning and natural language processing, to automate and streamline the recruitment process. From screening resumes to scheduling interviews, AI has been instrumental in making the recruitment process more efficient and objective.

One of the primary applications of AI in recruitment is in the screening of resumes. AI algorithms can swiftly scan through thousands of resumes, identifying key skills, experiences, and qualifications that match the job description. This not only saves time for recruiters but also minimizes human bias, ensuring that candidates are shortlisted based on merit and suitability for the role.

Another significant contribution of AI is in the realm of candidate engagement. AI-powered chatbots can interact with candidates, answering their queries, providing information about the company and the role, and even scheduling interviews. This enhances the candidate experience, ensuring that they feel valued and engaged throughout the recruitment process.

AI is also being used to predict candidate success. By analyzing data from various sources, AI can help recruiters assess a candidate's likelihood of success in a particular role. This predictive analysis can be a valuable tool in making informed hiring decisions.

However, while AI offers numerous benefits, it's important to be aware of its limitations. AI tools are only as good as the data they're trained on, and they may inadvertently perpetuate existing biases if the training data is biased. Moreover, AI cannot replace the human touch that is often crucial in the recruitment process.

As a job seeker, understanding AI's role in recruitment can help you navigate your job search more effectively. By tailoring your resume to include keywords relevant to the job description, engaging actively with AI chatbots, and being aware of the data-driven nature of recruitment, you can leverage AI to your advantage.

AI has transformed recruitment, making it more efficient, data-driven, and candidate-centric. As we navigate through a recession, embracing AI in our job-seeking journey can be a powerful strategy for success.

Staying Ahead of AI Trends in the Job Market

In the rapidly evolving landscape of the job market, Artificial Intelligence (AI) has emerged as a significant driver of change. As we navigate through economic downturns and recessions, understanding and staying ahead of AI trends can be a powerful strategy for career success.

One of the most notable trends is the increased demand for AI and Machine Learning skills. Companies across a wide array of sectors are recognizing the need to harness the power of these technologies, leading to a surge in opportunities for professionals equipped with these sought-after skills.

Interestingly, AI's influence is no longer confined to tech-centric firms. Industries that traditionally didn't have a strong tech focus, such as healthcare, finance, and transportation, are now integrating AI into their operations. This trend is creating a plethora of job opportunities in non-tech industries, broadening the scope for professionals with AI expertise.

As AI becomes more pervasive, there's a growing emphasis on its ethical implications. The rise of roles related to governance, ethics, and fairness of AI reflects this focus. Professionals who can navigate the complex ethical landscape of AI use are likely to be in high demand.

Another emerging trend is the notion of AI augmentation. The concept involves AI working alongside humans, complementing their abilities rather than replacing them. This shift is redefining jobs around human-AI collaboration, creating roles that didn't exist before.

With AI taking over routine tasks, soft skills such as problem-solving, creativity, and emotional intelligence are becoming more important. Employers are increasingly valuing professionals who can not only work effectively with AI but also bring these uniquely human skills to the table.

Finally, the focus on upskilling and reskilling for the AI-driven future of work is a trend that's here to stay. Companies are investing in training programs to equip their employees with necessary AI and machine learning skills, preparing them for the future.

In conclusion, as the field of AI continues to evolve rapidly, staying informed about these trends can provide you with a competitive edge. Whether you're looking to advance in your current role or transition to a new one, understanding how AI is shaping the job market can help you make informed career decisions, even during challenging economic times.

Chapter 5: Mastering the Application Process

Finding the right job can be a daunting task, but one of the most important steps in securing that dream role is mastering the application process. From crafting an effective resume to showcasing your qualifications and skills during interviews, understanding how to present yourself as a viable candidate is essential for success. This chapter will explore strategies for navigating the application process with confidence, from assessing your skillset and developing a growth mindset to building professional networks and crafting an effective personal brand. We'll also look at AI tools like ChatGPT that can give you a competitive edge when it comes to standing out among other applicants. Finally, we'll discuss online resources available for job seekers such as government-sponsored websites and applications.

Understanding Job Descriptions

In the challenging economic landscape of a recession, job hunting can feel like navigating through a dense forest. The key to finding your path lies in one crucial document – the job description. Understanding job descriptions is not just about reading the text but interpreting the underlying expectations and requirements that could set you apart as an ideal candidate.

What Is a Job Description?

A job description is more than a list of duties or responsibilities. It's a comprehensive snapshot of a role, providing insights into what the job entails, the skills it requires, and how it contributes to the broader organizational goals. The primary components of a job description include the job title, job purpose, job duties and responsibilities, required qualifications, preferred qualifications, and working conditions.

Decoding the Job Description

When reading a job description, it's crucial to approach it systematically. Start by giving the entire document a thorough read, treating it much like a comprehension exercise. This initial reading will give you a general sense of the role and whether it aligns with your career aspirations.

Next, delve deeper by looking at the qualifications and responsibilities. The qualifications section isn't just a checklist; it's a hierarchy of what the employer values most. Skills listed first are typically the most important, so ensure your resume reflects these skills prominently.

The responsibilities section outlines the core tasks the position entails. Pay close attention to the language used here. Phrases like "will be responsible for" or "must be able to" indicate mandatory requirements. If you can't fulfill these tasks, the job might not be a good fit.

Matching Titles and Responsibilities

Job titles can sometimes be misleading due to industry jargon or creative branding. Always base your understanding on the responsibilities outlined in the description rather than the job title alone. For instance, a 'Customer Happiness Specialist' might be a fancy term for 'Customer Service Representative'.

Reading Between the Lines

Job descriptions often contain subtle cues that hint at the company culture and expectations. For example, phrases like "fast-paced environment" or "flexible work hours" can imply a high-pressure job or a role that may require occasional overtime. Such insights can help you gauge whether the job fits your lifestyle and work ethic.

Utilizing the Job Description in Your Application
Lastly, use the job description to tailor your application and prepare for potential interviews. Highlight the skills and experiences that directly align with the job requirements. In your cover letter, address the job duties to demonstrate how your background prepares you to succeed in those areas.

During a recession, competition for jobs can be fierce. But by thoroughly understanding job descriptions, you can identify the right opportunities, tailor your applications effectively, and increase your chances of landing your dream job. Remember, every job description is a compass guiding you toward your next career move. So, read carefully, decode strategically, and navigate your path to success.

Tailoring Applications to Each Job

In the midst of a recession, the job market becomes increasingly competitive. As job seekers, it's crucial to stand out from the crowd, and one effective way to do this is by tailoring your applications for each job you apply to. This process involves aligning your resume and cover letter with the specific requirements and expectations outlined in the job description.

The Importance of Customized Applications

A common mistake job seekers make is sending generic resumes and cover letters to multiple employers. However, recruiters often screen hundreds of applications, so it's essential to make yours unique and relevant. A tailored application shows that you've taken the time to understand the role and the company, demonstrating your genuine interest and initiative.

Understanding the Job Description

Begin by thoroughly analyzing the job description. Identify key skills, qualifications, and responsibilities mentioned, and note any specific language or terminology used. These details will guide you in customizing your application materials.

61

Revamping Your Resume

Your resume should highlight your most relevant experiences and skills that match the job description. If a job requires expertise in a particular software, for example, ensure that your proficiency in this area is clearly stated on your resume.

While it's important to showcase your achievements, recruiters are more interested in how those achievements can benefit their company. Hence, frame your accomplishments in a way that demonstrates your potential value to the prospective employer.

Crafting a Compelling Cover Letter

Your cover letter offers an opportunity to elaborate on the experiences and skills mentioned in your resume. It should tell a story about your professional journey and how it aligns with the role you're applying for. Be sure to mention the company by name and discuss how your goals align with its mission and values. This not only shows that you've done your homework but also that you're enthusiastic about the opportunity.

Leveraging LinkedIn

In the digital age, your online presence can be as impactful as your resume or cover letter. Tailor your LinkedIn profile to mirror the changes you've made to your resume. Use the platform to showcase endorsements for your skills, recommendations from colleagues, and any relevant projects or publications.

The Follow-Up

After submitting your application, consider sending a follow-up email to reiterate your interest in the role. This can help keep your application top-of-mind for recruiters.

Tailoring your applications to each job can be time-consuming, but it's an investment that can significantly increase your chances of landing an interview, and ultimately, securing your dream job. In a recession, when competition is fierce, it's these strategic efforts that can set you apart from the crowd.

Standing Out in a Sea of Applicants

During a recession, competition for jobs can be intense, and standing out from the crowd is more important than ever. Here are some strategies to help you make your job application shine:

Tailor Your Application: Each job application should be customized to match the specific job description. Highlight the skills, experiences, and achievements that are relevant to the job you're applying for.

Showcase Transferable Skills: During a recession, flexibility is key. Highlight transferable skills that can be applied to various roles across industries. These might include communication, problem-solving, or leadership skills.

Network: Networking remains crucial, even during a recession. Reach out to industry professionals, attend virtual networking events, or join online industry groups. Networking can often lead to job opportunities that aren't publicly advertised.

Improve Your Online Presence: Make sure your LinkedIn profile is up-to-date and mirrors your CV. Use this platform to showcase endorsements, recommendations, and any relevant projects or publications.

Upskill: Use any downtime to upskill by taking online courses or gaining new certifications relevant to your industry. This shows employers your commitment to continual learning and development, even in challenging times.

Demonstrate Resilience: Employers value candidates who show resilience and adaptability, especially during a recession. Highlight instances where you've successfully navigated challenges or adapted to new circumstances.

Follow Up: After submitting your application, consider sending a follow-up email to reiterate your interest in the role. This can help keep your application top-of-mind for recruiters.

Remember, the goal is to not only secure a job but to find a role that suits your career ambitions and personal needs. By using these strategies, you can improve your chances of landing a job that's a good fit for you during a recession.

Tracking Your Applications

Amid a recession, job seekers often find themselves applying to numerous positions. This volume can quickly become overwhelming if not adequately managed. Hence, tracking your applications is a crucial strategy for maintaining organization and increasing your chances of success.

Why Track Your Applications?

Tracking your applications allows you to keep a record of the jobs you've applied for, the dates of application, the versions of your resume or cover letter used, and any follow-up actions. It can help prevent duplicate applications and ensure timely follow-ups. Moreover, it provides an overview of your job search progress, helping identify patterns or areas for improvement.

Creating an Application Tracker

An application tracker can be as simple as a spreadsheet. Key columns might include 'Company Name', 'Job Title', 'Date Applied', 'Resume Version', 'Cover Letter Version', 'Interview Dates', 'Follow-up Actions', and 'Outcome'.

Using Technology for Tracking

Several online tools can automate the tracking process. Job search platforms often have built-in features that allow you to track the jobs you've applied for. Alternatively, project management tools can be adapted for this purpose. Apps like Trello or Asana allow you to create boards for different stages of your job search, such as 'To Apply', 'Applied', 'Interview Stage', and 'Final Stage'.

Leveraging the Tracker for Follow-ups

A key benefit of tracking your applications is facilitating effective follow-ups. If you haven't heard back within two weeks of applying or one week after an interview, it's generally acceptable to follow up with the employer. Your tracker will provide all the necessary details at a glance, making this process efficient and timely.

Reflecting and Adapting

Your application tracker is not just a record; it's a tool for reflection and adaptation. If you're securing interviews for certain types of roles but not others, this could indicate where your skills and experience are most valued. If your applications rarely lead to interviews, it might be time to revise your resume or cover letter.

In a challenging job market, every application counts. By tracking your applications, you're not just staying organized; you're taking an active role in managing your job search and improving your chances of success. Remember, in a recession, the road to your dream job is often one of persistence and strategic adaptability.

Following up After Applying

In a recession, when competition for jobs is high, standing out from the crowd is crucial. One strategy that can set you apart is following up after applying. This shows your interest in the role and keeps your application fresh in the minds of recruiters.

Why Follow Up?

Following up serves multiple purposes. Firstly, it demonstrates your enthusiasm for the role and the company. Secondly, it ensures that your application has been received and hasn't been lost in a sea of other applications. Lastly, it puts your name back in front of the hiring manager, reminding them of your interest and qualifications.

When to Follow Up

Typically, waiting one to two weeks after submitting your application is a good rule of thumb. However, do pay attention to any guidance given in the job posting or during the application process. If they mention a specific timeline for hearing back, respect that.

How to Follow Up

The method of follow-up will depend on the contact information available. If an email address is provided, this is usually the best way to follow up. Keep your message concise, professional, and polite. Remind them of the position you applied for, express your continued interest, and inquire about the next steps.

For example:

Dear [Hiring Manager's Name],

I hope this email finds you well. I am writing to follow up on my application for the [Job Title] position at [Company Name]. I remain very interested in the opportunity and would appreciate any updates on the status of my application.

Thank you for considering my application. I look forward to the possibility of contributing to your team.

Best, [Your Name]

If you don't have an email address, a LinkedIn message or even a phone call might be appropriate. However, always err on the side of caution and respect the hiring manager's preferred methods of communication.

Following Up After an Interview

If you've had an interview, it's good practice to send a thank-you note within 24 hours. This not only shows your good manners but also reaffirms your interest in the role. You can then follow up again one week after the interview if you haven't heard anything.

Handling Rejection

If you follow up and learn that you haven't been selected, it's still beneficial to respond positively and professionally, thanking them for their time and asking them to keep you in mind for future opportunities. This leaves a positive impression and keeps the door open for future possibilities.

In a challenging economy, the job search process can often feel like a waiting game. But by taking the initiative to follow up, you're actively participating in your job hunt and increasing your chances of success. Remember, every step you take brings you closer to landing your dream job, even during a recession.

Chapter 6: Optimizing Resumes with AI

In today's competitive job market, having an effective resume is crucial for standing out from the crowd. But with employers receiving hundreds of applications for a single role, how can you differentiate yourself? The answer lies in leveraging AI-powered tools like ChatGPT to optimize your resume and gain an edge over other applicants. In this chapter, we'll explore how AI can be used to create resumes that stand out from the rest and help you land your dream job. We will discuss strategies such as assessing skills gaps, developing a growth mindset for continuous learning, crafting an effective personal brand, and utilizing online resources available to job seekers. Finally, we will bring together all the key points discussed in prior chapters into one concise conclusion emphasizing the impact of AI on job-seeking strategies during a recession.

The Role of AI in Resume Screening

In today's hyper-competitive job market, especially during a recession, landing your dream job is a complex process. One of the most significant innovations transforming this

70

process is Artificial Intelligence (AI). AI has revolutionized various industries, and its impact on the recruitment sector is profound. This chapter delves into the role of AI in resume screening, a vital step in the hiring process.

Understanding AI in Resume Screening

AI in resume screening is a technology that uses sophisticated algorithms to analyze resumes and extract key information such as work experience, skills, education, and other relevant details. This process goes beyond the traditional keyword-matching approach of an applicant tracking system, offering a more nuanced understanding of a candidate's potential fit for a role.

AI-powered resume screening tools can accurately identify qualified applicants, accelerating the hiring cycle and ensuring the most suitable candidates are not overlooked in the sea of applications. These tools help HR departments and recruiters save time, reduce human error, and minimize unconscious bias, ensuring a fair and efficient hiring process.

The Benefits of AI Resume Screening

AI resume screening offers considerable advantages, particularly in terms of time-saving and improved efficiency. By automating the initial resume screening and candidate evaluation, it allows recruiters to focus more on personalized interactions with potential candidates.

Moreover, AI reduces the risk of human errors and unconscious bias in the selection process, leading to more diverse and inclusive workplaces. It also enhances the quality of hires by making predictive analyses based on the data it processes, thus ensuring only the best-suited candidates progress to the interview stage.

Preparing Your Resume for AI Screening
To successfully navigate through AI resume screening, it's crucial to understand how these systems work. Here are some tips:

Use a clean, plain format: AI tools prefer simple, straightforward layouts. Avoid fancy templates or unusual formats that might confuse the system.

Include relevant keywords: AI screening tools look for specific keywords related to the job description. Make sure your resume includes these keywords, but avoid keyword stuffing.

Quantify your achievements: AI systems favor measurable achievements. Instead of stating you "increased sales," specify by how much, for instance, "increased sales by 20%."

Tailor your resume: Customize your resume for each job application. Match your skills and experiences to the job requirements.

Avoid errors: Ensure your resume is free from grammatical errors and typos as they could be red flags for AI systems.

Embracing the Future of Recruitment

As AI continues to evolve, it's clear that it will play an increasingly significant role in the recruitment process. As a job seeker navigating a challenging job market, understanding how AI works and how to make it work for you is crucial.

Embrace the changes brought about by AI in resume screening and use them to your advantage. By doing so, you'll increase your chances of securing your dream job, even in the toughest of times.

Creating an AI-Friendly Resume

In today's digital age, especially in times of economic recession, job seekers often find themselves competing against hundreds, if not thousands, of applicants for the same role. With the overwhelming number of resumes flooding in, more and more companies are turning to artificial intelligence (AI) to aid in their hiring process. Understanding how to create an AI-friendly resume can be your ticket to standing out in this competitive landscape and navigating your way to your dream job.

The Rise of AI in Recruitment

Artificial Intelligence is changing the face of recruitment, making the process more efficient and accurate. AI algorithms can sift through vast amounts of data in seconds, picking out the most relevant resumes based on predetermined criteria such as skills, experience, and education. This technology has proven invaluable during a recession when companies are keen to streamline operations and maximize efficiency.

Crafting an AI-Friendly Resume

Creating a resume that is friendly to AI screening requires strategic thinking and attention to detail. Here's how to make your resume appealing to both AI and human recruiters:

Focus on Keyword Optimization

One of the primary ways AI screens resumes is by scanning for industry-specific keywords and phrases. These keywords are often derived from the job description. Therefore, it's crucial to read the job posting carefully and incorporate relevant keywords into your resume naturally.

Don't Neglect the Basics

While AI is sophisticated, it still appreciates simplicity. Stick to traditional headings like 'Work Experience', 'Education', and 'Skills', and avoid getting creative with these. Additionally, always use a clean, easy-to-read font and layout.

Avoid Fancy Formatting

AI prefers simplicity when it comes to formatting too. Avoid using images, graphics, or unusual fonts as these can confuse the AI software. Also, refrain from putting important information in the header or footer as some AI systems may not recognize these sections.

Tailor Each Application

Just as you would tailor your cover letter for each job application, do the same with your resume. This doesn't mean rewriting your resume entirely each time, but tweaking it to align with the specific job description. This increases the chances of your resume containing the keywords that the AI is looking for.

Proofread Thoroughly

Finally, ensure there are no spelling or grammatical errors in your resume. AI, like human recruiters, doesn't respond favorably to sloppy mistakes.

Leveraging AI for Your Job Search

As AI continues to disrupt traditional recruitment practices, job seekers need to adapt their strategies to stay ahead. By creating an AI-friendly resume, you can increase your chances of making it past the initial screening stage, bringing you one step closer to landing your dream job, even during a recession.

Remember, while technology plays a significant role in the hiring process, the human element is still very much present. So, while optimizing your resume for AI, ensure it also appeals to the human recruiters who will ultimately make the hiring decision.

Using Keywords Effectively

Using keywords effectively in a job search during a recession is crucial to standing out among the competition and getting noticed by potential employers. Here's how you can do it:

Understand the Job Description: The job description is your primary source for understanding which keywords are important to a particular role. Look for specific skills, qualifications, duties, and other details that are emphasized. These are likely the keywords that employers will be looking for.

Use Industry-Specific Terms: Every industry has its own jargon and terminology. Be sure to include these in your resume and cover letters. This not only shows that you understand the industry but also helps your application get picked up by AI screening tools.

Incorporate Keywords Naturally: While it's important to include relevant keywords, it's equally important to use them naturally. Don't just list keywords—incorporate them into descriptions of your experiences and accomplishments.

Tailor Your Application: Each job is unique, so each application should be as well. Tailor your resume and cover letter to each job you apply for, using the keywords that are most relevant to that specific role.

Optimize Your Online Presence: Keywords aren't just for resumes and cover letters. They're also crucial for optimizing your LinkedIn profile and other online professional profiles. This can help recruiters find you when they search for potential candidates online.

Update Regularly: As you gain new skills and experiences, and as industry trends change, the keywords that are most relevant to you will change as well. Regularly update your resume, cover letter, and online profiles to reflect these changes.

Remember, the goal is to make it clear to potential employers that you have the skills and experiences they're looking for. By using keywords effectively, you can help them see this more easily, increasing your chances of landing a job, even in a challenging job market during a recession.

Highlighting Transferable Skills

In the challenging job market that often accompanies a recession, one of the most effective strategies for securing employment is to highlight your transferable skills. These are abilities you've gained through various experiences that can be applied to a wide range of jobs and industries.

Understanding Transferable Skills

Transferable skills are not industry-specific but are valuable across multiple fields and positions. They could be anything from communication and leadership to problem-solving and time management. These skills can be acquired from previous jobs, volunteer work, hobbies, sports, or even life experiences.

The Importance of Transferable Skills in a Recession During a recession, job opportunities in certain sectors may decrease significantly. However, with strong transferable skills, you can pivot and adapt to new opportunities in different sectors. Employers value these skills because they demonstrate your ability to add value in diverse roles and settings.

Moreover, transferable skills can set you apart from other candidates who may have specific industry experience but lack the broader skills that are applicable across various contexts.

How to Highlight Transferable Skills

To effectively highlight your transferable skills, you need to identify them, provide evidence of these skills, and present them strategically on your resume and during interviews.

Identifying Your Transferable Skills

Start by listing all your skills, then identify which ones are transferable. Reflect on your experiences in different areas of your life - work, education, volunteering, hobbies, and personal life. Think about the skills you used in these situations that could be useful in the job you're applying for.

Providing Evidence of Your Skills

Once you've identified your transferable skills, think of concrete examples where you've demonstrated these skills. This will provide evidence to support your claims and show employers how you've used these skills in real-world situations.

Presenting Your Skills Strategically

On your resume, incorporate your transferable skills into your experience descriptions rather than just listing them separately. This allows employers to see how you've applied these skills in context.

During interviews, use the STAR method (Situation, Task, Action, Result) to describe situations where you've used your transferable skills. This provides a clear narrative that illustrates your skills in action.

Embrace Your Transferable Skills

Highlighting your transferable skills is a powerful strategy for navigating your dream job during a recession. By identifying these skills and presenting them effectively, you can show potential employers that you're adaptable and capable of adding value in various contexts. In a volatile job market, this adaptability can be your greatest asset.

Showcasing Achievements Over Duties

In a challenging job market, particularly during a recession, it's crucial to make your resume stand out. One of the most effective ways to do this is by showcasing your achievements rather than simply listing your duties. This approach paints a picture of you as a proactive and results-oriented individual, which is highly attractive to potential employers.

Understanding the Difference Between Duties and Achievements

Duties refer to the tasks you were assigned in a particular role, while achievements are the outcomes or results of performing those tasks. While duties describe what you did, achievements highlight how well you did it and the impact you made.

For example, a duty might be 'Managed a team of sales professionals,' while an achievement would be 'Led a sales team that exceeded quarterly targets by 15% for four consecutive quarters.'

The Value of Highlighting Achievements

By focusing on achievements, you demonstrate to potential employers that you're not just capable of doing the job, but you can deliver significant results. This is especially crucial during a recession when companies are looking for employees who can contribute to their success in challenging times.

Moreover, achievements are concrete evidence of your skills and abilities. They show that you can apply your knowledge and expertise to make a positive impact, making you a valuable asset to any company.

How to Showcase Achievements Effectively

Showcasing achievements involves more than just stating what you've accomplished. It's about telling a compelling story of your professional journey. Here are a few strategies:

Use Action Verbs and Quantify Results

Start your achievement statements with strong action verbs like 'led', 'increased', 'developed', etc. Also, whenever possible, quantify your results to provide a clear picture of the scale and impact of your achievements.

Align Achievements with the Job Requirements

Your achievements should align with the requirements of the job you're applying for. This shows potential employers that you have a proven track record in areas that are critical to the role.

Provide Context

Provide enough context to ensure the employer understands the significance of your achievement. Explain the challenge you faced, the action you took, and the result of your action.

Make Your Achievements Shine

In a competitive job market, showcasing your achievements rather than just listing duties can set you apart. It's a powerful way to demonstrate your value and potential to prospective employers. By highlighting what you've accomplished, you're showing employers what you're capable of achieving for them, making you a compelling candidate even in a tough economic climate. Remember, in the quest for your dream job during a recession, your achievements are your most potent weapon.

Chapter 7: Crafting Compelling Cover Letters

In today's competitive job market, a well-written cover letter can be the difference between getting your foot in the door and being overlooked. It's an opportunity to introduce yourself to potential employers, build relationships with them, and explain why you are the ideal candidate for their vacancy. Crafting an effective cover letter requires creativity and strategic thinking, but it doesn't have to be difficult. In this chapter, we will look at how you can use AI tools like ChatGPT to create compelling cover letters that stand out from other applicants. We will also explore online resources such as government-sponsored websites and applications that can help you land your dream job during a recession.

The Purpose of a Cover Letter

In the pursuit of your dream job, especially during a recession, one tool often overlooked yet critical in your job search arsenal is the cover letter. A well-crafted cover letter can be your ticket to grabbing an employer's attention, even when job opportunities are scarce. So, what exactly is the purpose of a cover letter and why is it so important? Let's delve into this.

Understanding the Cover Letter

A cover letter is a one-page document typically accompanying your resume or CV. It is addressed to the interviewer or hiring manager, providing your contact details and the role you're applying for. But it's much more than just a formal introduction.

The cover letter is your opportunity to give a more detailed view of your accomplishments, qualifications, and interest in a position. While a resume shares the technical details of your skills and work experience, a cover letter gives insight into your soft skills, attitude, and motivations.

The Persuasive Power of a Cover Letter

As a piece of persuasive writing, your cover letter aims to convey to the employer why you're a great candidate for the role. It provides the opportunity to elaborate on what makes you uniquely qualified for the position and why you're applying for the role. Through this personalized explanation of your qualifications, you can connect with the employer on a deeper level, beyond the bullet points of your resume.

Making Your Case with a Cover Letter

The cover letter is tailored to the specific job you're applying for, highlighting how your qualifications relate to the job requirements. This customization shows your initiative, research, and genuine interest in the role and the company.

Your cover letter also serves to provide additional background information about your application. The goal of the cover letter is to highlight your best attributes, experiences, and achievements that align with the job description. It's your chance to tell a compelling story about your career journey and how it has led you to apply for the job at hand.

The Importance of a Cover Letter

During a recession, competition for jobs becomes more intense, and standing out from the crowd becomes even more crucial. A well-written cover letter can differentiate you from other candidates who may have similar qualifications. It can demonstrate your passion, commitment, and resilience—all desirable qualities in an uncertain economy.

In conclusion, the cover letter is not merely an optional add-on to your job application. It's a strategic tool that, if used effectively, can significantly enhance your chances of landing your dream job, even in a challenging economic climate. So, take the time to craft a thoughtful, engaging cover letter that showcases your unique value proposition to potential employers. It could make all the difference in navigating your way to success during a recession.

Example of a Cover Letter

[Your Name]
[Your Address]
[City, State, ZIP Code]
[Email Address]
[Phone Number]
[Date]

[Recipient's Name]
[Recipient's Job Title]
[Company Name]
[Company Address]
[City, State, ZIP Code]

Dear [Recipient's Name],

I am writing to express my keen interest in the [Job Title] position at [Company Name], as advertised on [Source of Advertisement]. With my strong passion for [relevant field or industry], combined with my extensive experience and skills, I believe I am an excellent fit for this role.

Throughout my career, I have demonstrated a consistent track record of delivering exceptional results and exceeding expectations. I have [number of years] years of experience in [specific field or industry], where I have honed my skills in [mention key skills relevant to the job]. I am confident in my ability to [mention key responsibilities or tasks relevant to the job] and contribute to the success of [Company Name].

What sets me apart is my ability to [mention a unique strength or achievement that aligns with the job requirements]. For example, in my previous role at [Previous Company], I successfully [describe a specific accomplishment or project that showcases your skills and abilities]. This experience has not only allowed me to develop a strong foundation in [mention specific skills], but it has also taught me the importance of [mention a value or principle important to the company culture].

Furthermore, I am highly adaptable and thrive in fast-paced environments. I possess excellent problem-solving abilities and have a proven ability to work well both independently and collaboratively as part of a team. I am also skilled in [mention relevant software or tools] and have a strong understanding of industry trends and emerging technologies.

I am truly excited about the opportunity to join [Company Name] and contribute to its continued success. I am impressed by the company's [mention a specific aspect or achievement of the company] and its commitment to [mention a value or principle important to the company culture]. I believe my skills, experience, and enthusiasm make me an ideal candidate for this role.

Thank you for considering my application. I have attached my resume for your review, which provides further details on my qualifications and accomplishments. I would welcome the chance to discuss how my skills align with the [Job Title] position and contribute to [Company Name]'s goals. I am available for an interview at your convenience and look forward to the opportunity to speak with you in person.

Thank you again for your time and consideration.

Sincerely,

[Your Name]

Addressing the Hiring Manager

In the competitive landscape of job hunting, especially during a recession, addressing your cover letter or email to the right person can make a world of difference. It is an art that requires attention to detail, research, and a bit of savvy. Let's explore how you can master this skill to stand out from the crowd and navigate your way toward your dream job.

The Importance of Personalization

Addressing the hiring manager directly establishes a personal connection and shows respect for their position. It demonstrates your initiative in finding out who is responsible for hiring and your dedication to making a good first impression. This level of personalization can set you apart from other applicants and help your application get noticed.

Finding the Hiring Manager's Name

The first step is finding the name of the hiring manager. This might require a bit of detective work. Start with the job posting. Sometimes, it will include the name of the person to whom you should address your application. If it doesn't, head over to the company's website. You might find the information you need on the 'About Us' or 'Our Team' page.

If the company's website doesn't reveal who the hiring manager is, LinkedIn can be a valuable resource. Search for the company and check out its employees. Look for people with titles like 'Recruiter', 'Hiring Manager', or something related to the department for which you're applying.

How to Address the Hiring Manager

Once you've found the hiring manager's name, use it to address them in your cover letter or email. It's best to use a formal, full-name salutation, such as "Dear John Doe," unless you know for sure that the company has a more casual culture. If you're unsure of the hiring manager's gender, it's safe to use their full name without a title.

If you are unable to find the hiring manager's name after exhausting all avenues, it's better to use a general salutation than to guess incorrectly. Phrases like "Dear Hiring Manager" or "Dear [Job Title] Team" are acceptable alternatives.

Crafting Your Message

Now that you've personalized your salutation, it's time to craft a compelling message. Begin by expressing your interest in the role and the company. Highlight your qualifications and how they align with the job requirements. Show enthusiasm, but keep it professional.

Remember, your goal is to convince the hiring manager that you're a strong fit for the position and the organization.

In conclusion, addressing the hiring manager directly in your job application is a small detail that can have a big impact. It shows respect, initiative, and attention to detail, qualities that are highly valued by employers, particularly in a recession. By mastering this subtle art, you'll be one step closer to landing your dream job.

Telling Your Story

As you navigate your job search during a recession, one key aspect that can distinctly set you apart from other candidates is your ability to tell your story. This narrative is a comprehensive view of your career journey, outlining your experiences, skills, values, and aspirations. So, how can you effectively tell your story to secure your dream job? Let's explore.

The Power of Storytelling in Job Search

Storytelling holds immense power in capturing attention and making an emotional connection. In the context of job search, your story provides potential employers with a clear picture of who you are, what you've accomplished, and where you aspire to go. It goes beyond the resume to present a holistic view of your career trajectory, reflecting your personality, passion, and potential.

Crafting Your Career Narrative

Begin by reflecting on your career path up till now. Identify the key milestones, turning points, achievements, and challenges. Think about the lessons learned, skills acquired, and the value you brought to your previous roles.

Next, consider your future. What are your career goals? What kind of role are you seeking? What are the values and mission that drive you? How do these align with the company or role you're applying for?

Now, weave these elements together into a cohesive narrative. Remember, a good story has a beginning, middle, and end. Start with your past (where you've been), move onto your present (where you are now), and then look to the future (where you want to go).

Communicating Your Story

Your career narrative should come through in every aspect of your job search. It should be evident in your resume, cover letter, LinkedIn profile, and job interviews.

In your resume and cover letter, use powerful action verbs and compelling language to describe your experiences and achievements. Show, don't just tell, the impact you've made in your past roles.

On LinkedIn, utilize the 'About' section to share a concise version of your career story. Highlight your key achievements, skills, and career goals.

During job interviews, use storytelling techniques to answer questions. For example, when asked about a certain skill or experience, share a specific instance from your past where you demonstrated that skill or gained that experience. This makes your response more memorable and impactful.

Navigating Recession with Your Story

During a recession, when competition for jobs is fierce, telling your story can be a game-changer. It allows you to show resilience, adaptability, and other qualities that are particularly valued in tough economic times. By sharing your unique career journey and aspirations, you can connect with potential employers on a deeper level, enhancing your chances of landing your dream job.

In conclusion, telling your story is an essential component of job searching. By crafting and communicating a compelling career narrative, you can stand out from the crowd and navigate your way toward success, even in a challenging economic climate.

Matching Your Skills to the Job

In the quest for your dream job, particularly during a recession, one of the most important strategies you can employ is effectively matching your skills to the job requirements. This alignment not only increases your chances of being selected for a job interview but also helps you stand out in a crowded job market. Let's explore how you can master this vital skill.

Understanding Job Requirements

The first step in matching your skills to a job is understanding the job requirements. These are usually outlined in the job description and may include technical skills, soft skills, and qualifications. Technical skills are job-specific skills required to perform a certain task or role. Soft skills, on the other hand, are interpersonal skills like communication, problem-solving, and leadership.

Understanding these requirements allows you to identify the skills you need to highlight in your application. It also gives you an idea of what the employer values most, helping you tailor your resume and cover letter accordingly.

Assessing Your Skills

Next, take inventory of your skills. This includes both the technical skills you've gained from your education and work experience, as well as the soft skills you've developed over time. Be sure to consider transferable skills—those skills that can be applied to various jobs across different fields, such as teamwork, organization, and time management.

Aligning Your Skills with the Job

Once you've identified the job requirements and assessed your own skills, it's time to align the two. Start by identifying which of your skills directly match the job requirements. These are your most relevant skills and should be prominently featured in your job application.

For each relevant skill, think of specific examples from your past experience where you've demonstrated that skill. These examples will provide evidence to support your claims and make your application more compelling.

Communicating Your Skills

Your resume, cover letter and job interviews are all platforms to communicate your skills. In your resume, use action verbs and quantifiable achievements to demonstrate your skills. In your cover letter, tell a story about how you've used a particular skill to achieve a positive outcome. During job interviews, use the STAR method (Situation, Task, Action, Result) to describe situations where you've utilized your skills.

Navigating a Recession with Skill Alignment

During a recession, when jobs are scarce and competition is high, effectively matching your skills to the job can give you an edge. It shows potential employers that you're not only qualified for the job, but also that you understand their needs and can add value to their organization.

Matching your skills to the job is a crucial strategy in securing your dream job. By understanding job requirements, assessing your skills, aligning the two, and effectively communicating your skills, you can navigate your way toward success, even in a challenging economic climate.

Ending on a High Note

In the journey towards your dream job, particularly during a recession, every interaction with potential employers is an opportunity to make a lasting impression. How you end these interactions—be it a cover letter, a job interview, or a networking conversation—can significantly influence your chances of success. Let's delve into how you can master the art of 'ending on a high note'.

The Importance of a Strong Ending

Psychological studies have shown that people tend to remember the end of an experience more vividly than the beginning or middle. This is known as the 'recency effect'. In the context of job search, this means that the way you conclude your interactions can leave a lasting impression on potential employers. A strong ending can reinforce your qualifications, show your enthusiasm, and make you more memorable.

Crafting a Powerful Conclusion in Your Cover Letter

Your cover letter is your initial introduction to potential employers. After outlining your skills and experiences, end your cover letter on a high note by expressing your enthusiasm for the role and the company. Clearly state your interest in contributing to the organization and your eagerness for the next steps in the hiring process. This positive ending can highlight your passion and commitment, making your application more compelling.

Leaving a Lasting Impression in Job Interviews

In job interviews, the closing moments are your final opportunity to make a strong impression. Use this time to reiterate your interest in the role and the value you can bring to the organization. Ask insightful questions that show your understanding of the company and the role. Finally, express your appreciation for the opportunity to interview and your excitement about the possibility of joining the team.

Ending Networking Conversations Positively

Networking is a valuable tool in job search, and ending these interactions positively can open doors to opportunities. When concluding a networking conversation, express gratitude for the person's time and insights. Share your excitement about your career prospects and your determination to succeed, even in a challenging economy. This positivity can leave a lasting impression, making you more memorable when opportunities arise.

Navigating a Recession with Positive Endings

During a recession, when competition for jobs is intense, ending on a high note can give you an edge. It shows potential employers that you're resilient, enthusiastic, and committed—qualities that are highly valued in uncertain times.

In conclusion, the way you conclude your interactions in your job search can have a significant impact on your prospects. By ending on a high note, you can leave a lasting impression that sets you apart from the crowd and brings you one step closer to securing your dream job, even in a challenging economic climate.

Chapter 8: Showcasing an Outstanding Portfolio

In the job market, showcasing an outstanding portfolio is key to standing out from the competition and gaining a competitive edge. A well-crafted portfolio can be instrumental in demonstrating your skills and capability to potential employers. In this chapter, we will discuss how you can create an impressive portfolio that showcases your talents and sets you apart from other job seekers. We'll look at strategies for highlighting your strengths, such as creating compelling visuals, curating relevant content, leveraging AI tools like ChatGPT, and using online resources available to job seekers. By the end of this chapter, you should have a better understanding of how to craft an outstanding portfolio that will help you land the job of your dreams!

Selecting Your Best Work

Amid a recession, showcasing an outstanding portfolio becomes even more important. It's not just about displaying your best work; it's also about demonstrating how you can deliver value in a tough economic climate. Here are some strategies for selecting your best work and building a portfolio that can withstand the trials of a recession.

Understand Your Goals and Risk Tolerance

Before you start selecting work for your portfolio, take a moment to decide your financial goals and their timeframes. Are you looking to secure a job immediately, or are you planning for long-term career growth? This will help you assess your tolerance for risk and losses. For instance, if you're aiming for quick employment, you might want to showcase work that appeals to a broad range of employers. But if you're focused on a particular industry or role, you may choose to highlight more specialized projects.

Diversify Your Portfolio

Just like an investment portfolio, your work portfolio should be diversified to demonstrate your versatility and adaptability. Include a variety of projects that showcase different skills and experiences. This could mean including work from different roles, industries, or types of projects. Not only does this show potential employers that you have a wide range of skills, but it also helps protect you against fluctuations in the job market.

Highlight Resilience and Adaptability

During a recession, employers are particularly interested in candidates who can thrive in challenging circumstances. Therefore, consider including work that demonstrates your resilience and adaptability. This could be a project where you had to overcome significant obstacles or an instance where you successfully adapted to changes in the market or industry.

Showcase Problem-Solving Skills

Recessions often bring complex problems that need innovative solutions. Highlighting work that showcases your problem-solving abilities can make you stand out to potential employers. This could be a project where you identified a unique solution to a difficult problem or an instance where your creative thinking led to significant improvements.

Think Before Rebalancing

Rebalancing your portfolio involves adding new work and removing older pieces to maintain a certain balance of skills or experiences. However, during a recession, it might be beneficial to keep some older work in your portfolio, especially if it demonstrates skills or experiences that are currently in demand.

Include Recession-Proof Work

If you have work that is relevant to industries that typically do well during recessions (such as healthcare, consumer staples, or utilities), be sure to include these in your portfolio. This shows potential employers that your skills are valuable, even in a challenging economic climate.

In conclusion, selecting your best work for a portfolio during a recession involves careful consideration of your goals, risk tolerance, and the current job market. By diversifying your portfolio, highlighting your resilience and problem-solving skills, and showcasing recession-proof work, you can create a portfolio that not only displays your best work but also positions you for success in a tough economic climate. Remember, the goal is not just to survive a recession, but to navigate it strategically in a way that sets you up for future success.

Organizing Your Portfolio

In the context of a recession, organizing and showcasing an outstanding portfolio becomes a vital step in navigating your dream job. This article will explore various strategies to curate and present a compelling portfolio that can stand strong during economic downturns.

Recognizing the Importance of a Well-Organized Portfolio

A well-organized portfolio is like a map guiding potential employers through your professional journey. It highlights your skills, experiences, and achievements in a structured and engaging manner. In a recession, when competition for jobs intensifies, a meticulously organized portfolio can set you apart from the crowd.

Aligning Portfolio with Your Career Goals

Your portfolio should be a reflection of your career aspirations. It should align with the industry or role you're targeting. For instance, if you're aspiring for a role in graphic design, your portfolio should predominantly showcase your design projects. This targeted approach can help you attract opportunities that fit your career goals, even during a recession.

103

Showcasing Versatility through Diversification

A diversified portfolio is a testament to your versatility. By including a variety of projects that demonstrate different skills and experiences, you show potential employers your adaptability—a highly sought-after trait, especially during a recession. This diversification can range from different roles, industries, to types of projects.

Emphasizing Resilience and Adaptability

Resilience and adaptability are two critical qualities that employers look for during a recession. By including projects where you've overcome significant challenges or adapted to changes efficiently, you can demonstrate these traits effectively. This not only makes your portfolio more appealing but also reassures potential employers of your ability to navigate through tough times.

Prioritizing Problem-Solving Skills

Recessions often bring complex problems that require innovative solutions. By highlighting projects that showcase your problem-solving skills, you can position yourself as a valuable asset who can contribute positively during challenging times.

Thoughtful Rebalancing of Your Portfolio

Your portfolio is not a static entity; it needs to evolve with your career progression and market demands. Rebalancing involves adding new work and removing older pieces to maintain a certain balance of skills or experiences. However, during a recession, you might want to retain some older work in your portfolio that demonstrates skills currently in demand.

Including Recession-Proof Work

Including work relevant to recession-resistant industries (like healthcare, consumer staples, or utilities) can make your portfolio more robust. It shows potential employers that your skills are valuable and applicable even in a challenging economic climate.

In conclusion, organizing your portfolio during a recession involves careful selection and presentation of your work. By aligning your portfolio with your career goals, showcasing versatility, emphasizing resilience and adaptability, prioritizing problem-solving skills, rebalancing thoughtfully, and including recession-proof work, you can create a compelling portfolio that helps you navigate toward your dream job amidst a recession.

Presenting a Variety of Skills

In the throes of a recession, your portfolio becomes your most potent tool. Showcasing a variety of skills in your portfolio can be the difference between blending in with the crowd and standing out to potential employers. This article delves into how you can effectively present a variety of skills in your portfolio during a recession.

The Power of a Diversified Skill Set

A diversified skill set is like a Swiss Army Knife – it equips you with the versatility to handle diverse situations, making you an invaluable asset to any employer. Especially during a recession, when companies are looking for employees who can wear many hats, a diversified skill set can significantly enhance your employability.

Aligning Skills with Industry Needs

The first step to presenting a variety of skills in your portfolio is to align them with the needs of the industry you're targeting. Research the skills in high demand in your desired industry and highlight these in your portfolio. This targeted approach can increase your chances of catching the attention of potential employers.

Demonstrating Adaptability and Resilience

Recessions are synonymous with change and uncertainty. In such times, adaptability and resilience become highly valued skills. Showcase projects or roles where you've had to adapt to new circumstances or bounce back from setbacks. This not only demonstrates your ability to withstand challenges but also your potential to thrive in them.

Showcasing Problem-Solving Abilities

In a recession, problem-solving abilities become even more crucial as companies face numerous challenges. Highlight instances where you've used creative thinking or innovative solutions to navigate complex problems. This can position you as a problem solver who can contribute positively to a company during tough times.

Highlighting Transferable Skills

Transferable skills, such as communication, leadership, and critical thinking, are valuable across industries and roles. Highlighting these skills in your portfolio can demonstrate your ability to perform various functions, making you an attractive candidate for a wide range of jobs.

Incorporating Recession-Proof Skills

If you possess skills relevant to industries that typically do well during recessions, like healthcare or utilities, make sure to feature these prominently in your portfolio. This can show potential employers that your skills are valuable and applicable, even in a challenging economic climate.

In conclusion, presenting a variety of skills in your portfolio involves careful selection and strategic showcasing of your capabilities. By aligning your skills with industry needs, demonstrating adaptability and resilience, showcasing problem-solving abilities, highlighting transferable skills, and incorporating recession-proof skills, you can build an outstanding portfolio that enhances your chances of navigating your dream job during a recession.

Keeping Your Portfolio Updated

During a recession, the job market becomes more competitive, and having an updated and relevant portfolio can be the key to securing your dream job. This article will delve into the importance of keeping your portfolio updated and how it ties into showcasing an outstanding portfolio during a recession.

The Significance of an Updated Portfolio

An updated portfolio is more than just a catalog of your recent work. It's a dynamic showcase of your growth, adaptability, and readiness to take on new challenges. In a recession, it serves as tangible proof of your ongoing relevance in a rapidly changing job market.

Staying Aligned with Industry Trends

Industries evolve, and so do the skills they value. By updating your portfolio regularly, you ensure that it reflects the current needs and trends of your target industry. This could involve adding projects that demonstrate newly acquired skills or removing outdated ones that no longer serve your career objectives.

Demonstrating Adaptability and Resilience

A recession brings change, uncertainty, and often, adversity. By updating your portfolio to include projects where you've successfully adapted or bounced back from setbacks, you can demonstrate your resilience. This not only enhances your portfolio but also signals to prospective employers your ability to thrive even in challenging circumstances.

Highlighting Your Problem-Solving Skills

In a recession, businesses face numerous challenges and are on the lookout for problem solvers. Regularly updating your portfolio to highlight instances where you've navigated complex problems or implemented innovative solutions can make you stand out. It shows potential employers that you're not just keeping pace with changes, but you're also equipped to contribute positively in tough times.

Incorporating Transferable and Recession-Proof Skills

Updating your portfolio also provides an opportunity to incorporate transferable skills and recession-proof skills. Transferable skills, such as leadership, communication, and critical thinking, are valuable across industries. On the other hand, recession-proof skills are those relevant to industries that usually remain stable or grow during recessions, like healthcare or utilities. Highlighting these skills in your updated portfolio can increase its appeal to a broader range of potential employers.

In conclusion, keeping your portfolio updated is crucial in showcasing an outstanding portfolio, especially during a recession. By aligning with industry trends, demonstrating adaptability, highlighting problem-solving skills, and incorporating transferable and recession-proof skills, you can maintain a portfolio that not only reflects your best and most relevant work but also positions you for success in a challenging job market.

Promoting Your Portfolio Online

During a recession, the job market becomes significantly more competitive. One way to stand out from the crowd and navigate toward your dream job is by effectively promoting your portfolio online. This article will provide insights on how to best showcase your portfolio online during an economic downturn.

The Power of Online Promotion

In today's digital age, your online presence can be just as important as your real-world one, if not more so. An online portfolio provides a platform where you can showcase your skills, experiences, and achievements to a global audience. In times of a recession, when job opportunities may be scarce, having a well-promoted online portfolio can open up avenues that might not be available otherwise.

Creating a Compelling Online Portfolio

The first step to promoting your portfolio online is to ensure that it is compelling and comprehensive. Make sure it includes your best work, demonstrates a variety of skills, and highlights projects where you've shown resilience and adaptability—traits that are especially valued during a recession. Also, remember to keep it updated with your latest work and achievements.

Leveraging Social Media

Social media platforms like LinkedIn, Twitter, Instagram, and Facebook are powerful tools for promoting your portfolio. They allow you to reach a wider audience, engage with potential employers, and stay connected with industry trends. You can share updates about new additions to your portfolio, discuss your work, and demonstrate your industry knowledge through posts and discussions.

Utilizing Portfolio Websites

There are numerous websites like Behance, Dribbble, or Squarespace, where you can create and host your portfolio. These platforms are frequented by recruiters and industry professionals, increasing the visibility of your work. Some of these sites also provide options to create a personalized URL, which you can include in your resume, social media profiles, and email signatures for easy access.

Engaging in Online Communities

Online communities, such as industry forums, LinkedIn groups, or Reddit threads, can be effective venues for promoting your portfolio. Participating in discussions, offering advice, and sharing your work in these communities can help establish your reputation and draw attention to your portfolio.

Optimizing for Search Engines

Search Engine Optimization (SEO) can increase the visibility of your online portfolio. This involves using relevant keywords in your portfolio's content and meta descriptions, ensuring your website is mobile-friendly, and regularly updating your portfolio with fresh content.

In conclusion, promoting your portfolio online is crucial in showcasing an outstanding portfolio, particularly during a recession. By creating a compelling online portfolio, leveraging social media, utilizing portfolio websites, engaging in online communities, and optimizing for search engines, you can increase the visibility of your work, connect with potential employers, and navigate successfully toward your dream job, even in challenging economic times.

Chapter 9: Excelling in the Interview Stage

The interview stage of the job search process is an important step for both employers and applicants. It allows employers to get a better sense of the applicant's personality, skills, and abilities, while also giving applicants the chance to demonstrate their qualifications in person. However, succeeding at this stage can be difficult without preparation and practice. In this chapter, we will explore strategies for excelling in interviews by researching companies ahead of time, using body language effectively during interviews, developing creative solutions to problems posed by potential employers, and more. With these tips in hand, you'll be able to confidently make your case as a valuable addition to any team!

Preparing for Common Questions

The interview stage is a critical part of any job search, but it takes on even more significance during a recession. With companies often tightening their belts and looking for the most adaptable and resilient candidates, it's important to be prepared for the questions that will come your way.

Interviewers will likely focus on your past work experiences, particularly those that relate to the role you're applying for. They'll want to know why you think you'll succeed in this position - a question designed to evaluate your relevant skills and understanding of the job.

Adaptability is another key trait that interviewers look for, particularly in a challenging economic climate. You may be asked about the biggest change your previous company or department has gone through in the last year, allowing you to showcase your ability to navigate and thrive amidst change.

One of the most basic yet significant questions you'll face is, "Could you please tell me about yourself?" This is your chance to highlight your resilience and problem-solving abilities, both of which are highly valued during a recession.

Your motivations for seeking a new role will also be scrutinized. If asked, "Why are you making a move in this economic climate?" be prepared to explain your reasons clearly and convincingly, demonstrating that you're not merely a risk-taker, but a calculated one.

The question, "What do you consider to be your ideal job?" or "Do you like having a boss, or do you like being your own boss?" can reveal a lot about your career aspirations and working style. Make sure your answers align with the company's culture and the nature of the role you're applying for.

Finally, don't forget to ask your own questions. For instance, "Did the company have layoffs when Covid-19 shut down the country?" or "Have supply chain issues impacted the business?" These can help you assess the company's stability and crisis management capabilities.

In addition to these, here are 10 more sample questions you might encounter:

1. "How do you handle stress and pressure?"
2. "How do you prioritize your work?"
3. "What are your salary expectations?"
4. "Why should we hire you?"
5. "How do you handle failure?"
6. "What are your long-term career goals?"
7. "How do you define success?"
8. "How do you handle feedback and criticism?"
9. "Can you describe a difficult work situation and how you overcame it?"
10. "What are your strengths and weaknesses?"

Remember, an interview is not just about answering questions; it's also an opportunity to demonstrate your value, flexibility, and commitment. Preparation is key to excelling in this stage and moving one step closer to landing your dream job, even in a recession.

Researching the Company

Researching a company prior to an interview can provide you with valuable insights, helping you excel during the interview stage. It allows you to tailor your responses to

116

align with the company's values, culture, and goals, thereby demonstrating to the interviewer that you're a great fit for their organization.

Here are some strategies for researching a company:

Exploring the Company Website

The company's official website is usually the best place to start your research. Pay attention to the mission statement, history, and any recent news or updates. The 'About Us' section can provide you with a good understanding of the company's values and culture.

Using Google News

Google News can help you find recent developments about the company. This could include new product launches, executive changes, major projects, or controversies. Being aware of these can help you ask informed questions during the interview and show that you've done your homework.

Reviewing Social Media Accounts

The company's social media accounts can provide a wealth of information. They can give you a sense of the company's brand voice, how they interact with their customers, and what issues matter to them. LinkedIn can be particularly useful for understanding the company's industry presence and getting a sense of who you might be working with.

Checking Company Reviews

Websites like Glassdoor and Indeed can offer employee reviews of the company. While it's important to take these with a grain of salt, they can still give you a sense of what current and past employees think of the company.

Understanding Their Products/Services

Having a thorough understanding of the company's products or services is crucial. Not only will this help you answer questions during the interview, but it also allows you to demonstrate enthusiasm for what the company does.

Remember, the goal of your research is not just to gather information, but to use that information to present yourself as the best candidate for the job. By showing that you understand and align with the company's values and goals, you'll be well-positioned to excel in the interview stage.

Dressing for Success

The way you dress for an interview can have a significant impact on the impression you make. It's not simply about looking good; it's about presenting a professional image that aligns with the company's culture and values. In the midst of a recession, when competition is high, dressing for success becomes even more crucial.

Dressing professionally for all interviews, regardless of the company's dress code, is a key element of making a positive impression. Your attire should show that you've taken the time to prepare and that you respect the interviewer and the company.

Choosing your interview outfit the night before can help reduce stress on the day of the interview. It allows you to ensure that your clothing is clean, wrinkle-free, and appropriate for the company you're interviewing with.

Attention to detail can set you apart from other candidates. This includes ensuring your shoes are polished, your clothes are well-fitted and not distracting, and any accessories are subtle and professional.

When deciding what to wear, consider the company's culture. For traditional corporate organizations, a suit in a neutral color such as navy blue or black is typically a safe choice. However, if you're interviewing at a less conservative company or one that values creativity, you might choose a statement dress paired with a complementary blazer, or a pair of well-fitted slacks and a stylish blouse.

Remember, the goal is to let your skills and experiences take center stage, not your clothes. Dress in a way that makes you feel confident and comfortable, allowing you to focus on the interview itself.

In conclusion, dressing for success is a critical part of excelling in the interview stage. By carefully considering your outfit and ensuring it matches the company's culture and expectations, you'll be well-positioned to make a positive and lasting impression.

Making a Positive Impression

In the pursuit of your dream job during a recession, making a positive impression at the interview stage is paramount. This chapter will guide you on how to excel at this critical stage and leave a lasting impression that sets you apart from other candidates.

Navigating an interview successfully starts with preparation. This includes researching the company thoroughly. Delve into the company's history, mission, values, and recent developments. This information will not only equip you to answer questions more effectively but will also demonstrate to the interviewer your genuine interest in the company and its future.

Next, prepare for common interview questions. Anticipate what might be asked and practice your responses. Remember, your answers should go beyond just explaining your skills and experiences; they should highlight how you can bring value to the company, especially during challenging economic times.

Dressing appropriately for the interview also plays a crucial role in making a positive impression. Your attire should reflect the company's culture and show that you respect the interview process. Always lean towards professional attire, ensuring your clothes are neat, clean, and conservative.

The way you communicate during the interview can significantly impact the impression you make. Be confident, maintain eye contact, listen attentively, and respond thoughtfully. Show enthusiasm for the role and the company, and don't forget to ask insightful questions. This shows that you're engaged and genuinely interested in the opportunity.

After the interview, follow up with a thank-you note. This simple gesture can help reinforce your interest in the position and show your appreciation for the interviewer's time. It's another opportunity to leave a positive impression and differentiate yourself from other candidates.

In a recession, the competition for jobs can be fierce. By making a strong positive impression during the interview stage, you increase your chances of standing out from the crowd and moving closer to securing your dream job. Remember, every interaction with a potential employer is an opportunity to showcase your professionalism, competence, and enthusiasm for the role.

Asking Your Own Questions

In a job interview during a recession, asking effective questions can not only help you stand out as a candidate but also provide you with crucial insights into the company's stability and future prospects. Here are some strategies and examples of effective questions to ask:

1. Understand the Company's Stability: You'll want to gauge how the company has been affected by the recession and what its plans are for the future. You might ask, "Can you share how the company has adapted to the current economic climate?" or "What strategies has the company implemented to navigate through this recession?"

2. Assess Job Security: Given the uncertainties of a recession, it's important to get a sense of the role's security. Questions like, "How has this position evolved during the recession?" or "How does this role contribute to the company's long-term goals?" can offer valuable insights.

3. Evaluate the Company's Culture: Understanding how the company treats its employees during challenging times can reveal a lot about its culture. Consider asking, "Can you share any measures the company has taken to support its employees during this recession?"

4. Learn About Growth Opportunities: Even in a recession, you'll want to grow professionally. Ask questions like, "What opportunities for professional development does the company offer?" or "How has the company supported employee growth and advancement during this period?"

5. Uncover Expectations: It's essential to understand what will be expected of you, especially during a challenging economic period. Ask, "What are the key priorities for this role in the next six months?" or "How will my performance be evaluated?"

Remember, your questions should demonstrate your interest in the role, your understanding of the current economic climate, and your ability to contribute to the company's success during a recession.

Chapter 10: AI-Powered Market Analysis and Research

In today's competitive job market, it is essential to stay ahead of the curve. To do this, you need to be able to quickly and accurately analyze and research the current market conditions. Fortunately, artificial intelligence (AI) tools can help you gain a competitive edge by providing insights into labor trends and helping you assess your skills for those of other candidates. In this chapter, we will explore how AI-powered market analysis and research can give job seekers an advantage during a recession. We'll discuss AI tools such as ChatGPT that enable faster data processing and more accurate predictions about future labor markets, as well as online resources for job seekers including government-sponsored websites and applications. Finally, we'll bring together all the key points from prior chapters in a concise manner so that you have everything you need to navigate the challenging job landscape with confidence!

Leveraging AI for Market Research: A Guide to AI-Powered Market Analysis and Research

In today's fast-paced business environment, the power of artificial intelligence (AI) in reshaping market research can't be overstated. As we navigate through an economic recession, understanding the role AI plays in market analysis becomes vital for anyone seeking their dream job. This chapter aims to shed light on how AI is transforming market research and how you can leverage it for your success.

The Power of AI in Market Research

AI is revolutionizing the field of market research with its incredible ability to process enormous volumes of data, identify patterns and trends, and generate actionable insights. According to a Qualtrics report, 93% of researchers see AI as an industry opportunity, while 80% believe it will positively impact the market-research industry.

AI-powered tools enhance data collection and improve analysis capabilities, providing businesses with accurate and timely information on customer behavior. This allows for more targeted marketing strategies, ultimately leading to better engagement with the target audience.

AI algorithms also hold the key to redefining the market research industry by eliminating outmoded dynamics. They address factors like reducing costs, increasing efficiency, and enhancing the overall quality of research.

Practical Ways to Leverage AI in Market Research

Let's explore some practical ways you can leverage AI in your market research efforts:

Understanding Emotions: AI technologies like facial coding and sentiment analysis can help businesses understand the emotional response their products or services elicit, enabling them to make data-driven decisions about product development, branding, and marketing strategies.

Targeting Audiences: AI can collect user data and use it to develop insights about consumer preferences and behaviors. This allows businesses to find the right consumers and engage with them effectively.

Conducting ROI Analysis: AI can automate the process of return-on-investment analysis, saving time and resources while providing valuable insights about the effectiveness of different marketing strategies.

Identifying Trends: AI can examine data from customers and social media platforms to identify emerging trends, giving businesses a competitive edge.

Improving Efficiency: AI can automate repetitive tasks, freeing up researchers to focus on more important responsibilities.

Navigating Your Dream Job in a Recession with AI

Leveraging AI in market research isn't just beneficial for businesses. It's also a critical skill for job seekers, especially during a recession. Understanding AI and its applications in market research can make you a valuable asset to potential employers.

As businesses strive to stay competitive during tough economic times, they need employees who understand how to leverage AI to make informed decisions. By mastering AI-powered market research, you can position yourself as a strategic thinker capable of guiding a business through a recession.

In conclusion, the role of AI in market research is becoming increasingly important. Whether you're a business owner looking to gain a competitive edge or a job seeker trying to stand out in a tough job market, understanding and leveraging AI can be your ticket to success. As we navigate through this recession, let's harness the power of AI to create effective strategies and achieve our goals.

Using AI to Identify Industry Trends

In the challenging landscape of an economic recession, finding your dream job requires more than just skill and perseverance. It demands a deep understanding of industry trends and the ability to navigate them effectively. In this context, Artificial Intelligence (AI) emerges as a powerful ally. This chapter will delve into how AI can be used to identify industry trends, aiding in your quest for your dream job amidst a recession.

The Power of AI in Identifying Industry Trends

AI has revolutionized the way we interpret data, providing insights that were previously inaccessible due to the sheer volume and complexity of information available. Whether it's predicting consumer behavior, identifying emerging markets, or forecasting economic shifts, AI algorithms can provide insights far beyond the capability of traditional research methods.

One of the most significant advantages of AI is its ability to process and analyze massive amounts of data swiftly and accurately. This ability enables AI to identify patterns and trends that might be invisible to the human eye. For example, AI can analyze social media posts, online reviews, and other digital data to identify trends in consumer behavior, market demand, and industry shifts.

AI-Powered Market Analysis and Research

The use of AI in market analysis and research has grown exponentially in recent years. Tools such as Brandwatch Consumer Intelligence, TalkWalker, Qlik Sense, Microsoft Power BI, Meltwater, IBM Cognos Analytics, and others have been developed to harness the power of AI in analyzing market trends.

These tools use AI to gather, analyze, and interpret data from various sources, offering valuable insights about the market. They can identify trends in consumer behavior, predict future market movements, and provide comprehensive market analysis reports. This information can be invaluable for anyone looking to secure their dream job in a challenging economic climate.

Navigating Your Dream Job During a Recession with AI

During a recession, companies are on the lookout for employees who can bring value and drive growth. Understanding industry trends and being able to predict future market movements is a highly sought-after skill. And this is where your knowledge of AI-powered market analysis can set you apart.

By leveraging AI tools, you can gain insights into the market trends of the industry you're interested in. You can understand what consumers want, where the industry is heading, and what skills are in high demand. This knowledge can help you tailor your job applications, ace your interviews, and secure your dream job.

Moreover, understanding AI itself is a valuable skill. As more and more companies incorporate AI into their operations, having a solid grasp of AI and its applications can make you a desirable candidate.

AI offers a powerful tool for identifying industry trends and navigating the job market during a recession. By harnessing the power of AI, you can gain a competitive edge, making you stand out amongst other candidates and bringing you one step closer to landing your dream job.

Predictive Analysis for Job Hunting

In the uncertain landscape of a recession, job hunting can seem daunting. However, the rise of Artificial Intelligence (AI) and predictive analysis presents an opportunity for job seekers to navigate this challenge with greater ease and precision. This chapter from 'Navigating Your Dream Job: Strategies for Success During a Recession' explores how predictive analysis can be leveraged for job hunting, particularly in understanding industry trends.

The Power of Predictive Analysis in Job Hunting

Predictive analysis, an application of AI, involves using historical data to forecast future outcomes. In the context of job hunting, predictive analysis can provide insights into hiring trends, skill demands, salary expectations, and more. It is an invaluable tool for job seekers, especially during a recession when competition for jobs is high and opportunities may be scarce.

Predictive analysis uses machine learning algorithms to analyze large volumes of data, including job postings, resumes, and employment trends. This data-driven approach can identify patterns and trends that can guide job seekers. For instance, it can predict which industries are likely to grow despite the economic downturn or which skills are in high demand.

Using AI to Identify Industry Trends

AI plays a crucial role in identifying industry trends, which is vital for job hunting during a recession. By analyzing data from various sources, including social media, news articles, company reports, and job postings, AI can identify emerging trends in different industries.

For example, AI can detect an increase in remote work opportunities or a growing demand for digital marketing skills. This information allows job seekers to tailor their applications and develop relevant skills, increasing their chances of securing a job.

Moreover, tools like LinkedIn's Talent Insights harness AI to provide data-driven insights about labor market trends, helping job seekers understand where opportunities lie.

Understanding and leveraging predictive analysis and AI can be instrumental in navigating your dream job during a recession. These technologies provide actionable insights that can guide your job search strategy.

By understanding industry trends, you can align your skills and experiences with the needs of the market. Predictive analysis can help you anticipate changes in the job market, allowing you to adapt and stay ahead of the competition.

Furthermore, knowledge of AI and predictive analysis is a valuable skill in itself. As businesses increasingly incorporate these technologies, professionals with an understanding of AI and data analysis are highly sought after.

In conclusion, predictive analysis and AI offer powerful tools for job hunting during a recession. By providing insights into industry trends and future predictions, they enable job seekers to navigate the job market strategically and effectively. As we face the challenges of a recession, let's harness the power of technology to carve our path to success.

AI in Competitive Analysis

In the modern business landscape, Artificial Intelligence (AI) is making significant strides in many areas, including competitive analysis. As we navigate through a recession, understanding how AI can be used to analyze competitors and identify industry trends becomes increasingly crucial. This chapter explores the role of AI in competitive analysis, providing valuable insights for job seekers in these challenging times.

The Power of AI in Competitive Analysis

Competitive analysis refers to the process of identifying your competitors and evaluating their strategies to determine their strengths and weaknesses relative to your own. AI has revolutionized this process by enabling businesses to analyze vast amounts of data quickly and accurately, providing insights that were previously inaccessible due to the sheer volume and complexity of the information available.

AI-powered competitive analysis tools like Crayon and Kompyte can monitor competitors' online activities in real-time, tracking changes in pricing, product development, marketing campaigns, and more. They use machine learning algorithms to analyze this data and identify patterns and trends, providing businesses with actionable insights to inform their strategic decisions.

AI in Identifying Industry Trends

Understanding industry trends is critical for anyone looking to secure their dream job during a recession. These trends can provide insights into the direction the industry is heading, the skills that are in demand, and the opportunities that are likely to arise in the future.

AI can analyze data from various sources, including social media, news articles, market reports, and job postings, to identify emerging trends in different industries. For example, AI can detect an increase in remote work opportunities, a growing demand for digital marketing skills, or a shift toward sustainable business practices. This information can guide job seekers in tailoring their applications, developing relevant skills, and navigating their career paths during a recession.

In a recession, the job market becomes more competitive, and understanding the competitive landscape of your industry is key to standing out from the crowd. By leveraging AI in competitive analysis, job seekers can gain insights into the strategies of successful companies, the trends shaping the industry, and the skills that employers are looking for.

Moreover, knowledge of AI itself is becoming a highly sought-after skill. As more businesses incorporate AI into their operations, professionals who understand how to use

AI to analyze data and generate insights are in high demand.

In conclusion, AI offers a powerful tool for competitive analysis and identifying industry trends. For those seeking their dream job during a recession, understanding and leveraging AI can provide a competitive edge, helping them navigate the challenges of the job market and carve a successful career path.

Understanding Data Privacy and Ethics

In today's data-driven world, Artificial Intelligence (AI) is a powerful tool for identifying industry trends and navigating the job market, especially during a recession. However, as we leverage the power of AI, it's crucial to understand the importance of data privacy and ethics. This chapter explores these concepts, providing valuable insights for anyone seeking their dream job in these challenging times.

The Intersection of AI, Data Privacy, and Ethics

AI can analyze vast amounts of data quickly and accurately, making it an invaluable tool for identifying industry trends. However, this capability also raises significant concerns about data privacy and ethics. As AI systems collect, store, and analyze data, it's crucial to ensure that they do so in a manner that respects individual privacy rights and adheres to ethical standards.

Data privacy refers to the right of individuals to control how their personal information is collected and used. In the context of AI, this means ensuring that data is collected with

134

consent, stored securely, and used for its intended purpose. Failure to respect data privacy can lead to breaches of trust, legal penalties, and damage to a company's reputation.

Ethics in AI, on the other hand, involves ensuring that AI systems are designed and used in a manner that is fair, transparent, and accountable. This includes addressing issues such as bias in AI algorithms, transparency in how AI systems make decisions, and accountability for the outcomes of these decisions.

The Role of Data Privacy and Ethics

Understanding data privacy and ethics is not only crucial for businesses using AI but also for job seekers. As companies increasingly incorporate AI into their operations, professionals who understand the importance of data privacy and ethics are in high demand.

Moreover, as AI becomes more integrated into the job market, job seekers need to consider how their data is being used. For example, AI-powered recruitment tools may analyze your resume, online profile, or even your social media posts to assess your fit for a job. Understanding your data privacy rights can help you navigate these situations and ensure that your personal information is being used appropriately.

Furthermore, understanding ethics in AI can help job seekers identify companies that align with their values. Companies that prioritize ethical AI use are likely to have a strong commitment to fairness, transparency, and accountability, which are important qualities in an employer.

In conclusion, as we navigate the challenges of a recession and leverage AI to identify industry trends, it's crucial to understand the importance of data privacy and ethics. By doing so, we can ensure that we're not only using AI effectively but also responsibly.

Chapter 11: Virtual Interview Skills

As the job market becomes more competitive, employers are increasingly relying on virtual interviews to assess potential candidates. This chapter will provide an overview of what to expect from a virtual interview and strategies for succeeding in this format. We'll cover topics such as how to prepare for an online interview, best practices for communicating effectively over video calls, tips for showcasing your skills and experience, and techniques for standing out from the competition. With these guidelines in hand, you'll be able to demonstrate your value during a virtual interview with confidence and poise.

Setting Up Your Space

Setting up a space for virtual interviews involves creating an environment that is both professional and free from distractions. Here are some tips based on the search results:

Organize Your Space: Ensure your space is clean and tidy. A cluttered background can be distracting and give off a poor impression.

Log on Early: This will allow you to troubleshoot any technical issues that may arise and ensure you're ready when the interview starts.

Ensure Your Audio Works: Test your microphone before the interview to make sure the interviewer can hear you.

Look at the Camera: Eye contact is important in interviews, so try to look directly at the camera when you're speaking.

Don't Use Virtual Backgrounds: They can often look unprofessional and distract from the conversation. Instead, opt for a simple, real-life background.

Choose Your Lighting Carefully: Position yourself in a well-lit area that isn't in direct sunlight. Natural light is often the most flattering, so if possible, set up across from a window.

Prepare for the Unexpected: Have a plan in case something goes wrong like your internet connection dropping out.

Rehearse: Practice makes perfect. Consider doing a mock interview to get comfortable with the format.

Set the Scene: Your video call setup can make a great first impression. Consider what your background says about you and adjust accordingly.

Turn Off Notifications: Open up necessary websites and documents you'll want to access during the meeting and turn off notifications for at least two hours so no one interrupts you.

Remember, the goal is to create a space where you can focus on the interview and present yourself in the best possible light.

Mastering Video Call Etiquette

As we navigate the modern job market, particularly during economic downturns, virtual interviews have become a commonplace method for employers to assess potential employees. This transition from face-to-face to digital interaction calls for a fresh set of decorum rules to be observed. In this chapter, we delve into the art of mastering video call etiquette, a vital component of your virtual interview skills that can guide you toward securing your dream job, despite a recession.

Getting to Know the Platform

Mastering video call etiquette begins with gaining a comprehensive understanding of the platform being used for your interview. Whether it's Zoom, Microsoft Teams, or Google Meet, ensure you're familiar with how to operate key features like muting/unmuting your microphone, activating/deactivating your camera, sharing your screen, and utilizing the chat feature. A practice run with a friend or family member can help you identify and rectify any technical issues ahead of the actual interview.

Creating Your Space

Establishing a professional environment free from distractions is crucial for a successful virtual interview. Choose a quiet, well-lit area where interruptions will be minimized. Aim for a tidy, neutral backdrop; a chaotic or busy background can detract from your interview. If finding such a space proves challenging, consider using a tasteful virtual background.

Dressing for Success

Regardless of the virtual nature of the interview, maintaining professionalism in your attire remains important. Dress as though you were attending an in-person interview, steering clear of overly bright or patterned clothing that may distract on camera. The use of headphones can enhance audio quality and lessen the likelihood of echo or feedback.

Maintaining Eye Contact

Just as in a traditional interview, eye contact carries significant weight in a virtual setting. Looking directly into the camera conveys confidence and respect. Avoid the temptation to look at your image on the screen, as this can give the impression that you're not maintaining eye contact with the interviewer.

Handling Technical Difficulties

Technical hiccups are sometimes unavoidable, but your approach to handling them can showcase your problem-solving capabilities. If an issue arises, stay composed, communicate the problem succinctly, and endeavor to resolve it promptly. If the problem continues, suggest the possibility of rescheduling or switching to a phone call.

Effective Communication

Ensure you speak clearly and allow for regular pauses to prevent talking over the interviewer. Make a habit of muting your microphone when not speaking to reduce any potential background noise.

By honing these video call etiquette skills, you position yourself as a proficient, professional candidate equipped to tackle any challenge, including securing your dream job amidst a recession.

Overcoming Technical Difficulties in Virtual Interviews

In the digital age, and particularly during a recession, virtual interviews have become a standard part of the job-hunting process. They provide a convenient way for employers to meet with potential candidates without the constraints of location or travel. However, these interviews also introduce a new set of challenges: technical difficulties. This chapter will focus on how to overcome these hurdles, ensuring you present your best self in any virtual interview setting, even in the face of unexpected issues.

Preparation is Key

The first step towards overcoming technical difficulties is to prepare in advance. Familiarize yourself with the platform being used for the interview, whether it's Zoom, Skype, Google Meet, or another video conferencing software. Understand how to use essential features like muting and unmuting your microphone, turning your camera on and off, sharing your screen, and using the chat function. Conducting test runs with friends or family members can help you identify potential issues before they arise in the actual interview.

Troubleshoot Your Technology

Ensure your technology is up to the task. Check your internet connection for stability and speed. If your current setup isn't reliable, consider alternatives like using a wired connection instead of Wi-Fi or finding a different location with a stronger connection. Test your webcam and microphone for quality and familiarity with their settings. Always have a backup plan, such as a secondary device ready to go, in case your primary device fails.

Handling Glitches Gracefully

Despite your best preparation, technical glitches may still occur. How you handle them can leave a lasting impression on your prospective employer. Stay calm and communicate clearly about the issue at hand. Most interviewers will understand, as they're likely familiar with the challenges of technology too. If the problem persists, suggest rescheduling the interview or switching to a phone call. This shows your adaptability and problem-solving skills, traits highly valued in any employee.

Keep Software and Hardware Updated

Regular updates to your devices and applications can prevent many technical issues from happening. Running the latest versions of your operating system and video conferencing software ensures you have the most recent bug fixes and improvements, leading to a smoother interview experience.

Ask for Help

If you're unsure about any aspect of the technology involved in a virtual interview, don't hesitate to ask for help. Reach out to tech-savvy friends, family members, or even the company's IT department. They can provide guidance and help you feel more comfortable with the technology.

Mastering the art of overcoming technical difficulties in virtual interviews is an essential skill in the modern job market. By taking these steps, you'll be well-prepared to navigate your dream job interview, even during a recession.

Communicating Clearly Online

In today's digital world, and especially during a recession, virtual interviews have become the standard. Companies are leveraging technology to connect with potential candidates, making it essential for job seekers to develop strong online communication skills. This chapter will delve into the art of communicating online, a crucial aspect of virtual interview skills, as we navigate towards landing our dream job amidst economic challenges.

Understanding the Medium

Online communication is different from face-to-face interaction. The lack of physical presence can make it harder to read cues and convey nuances. It's essential to understand this medium to ensure your messages are clear and effective. Familiarize yourself with the platform you'll be using for the interview and its features, such as muting/unmuting, camera controls, and screen sharing.

Concise and Clear Messaging

In a virtual interview, being concise and clear is paramount. Ensure your responses are direct and to the point, without unnecessary jargon or lengthy explanations. Keep your language simple, making it easier for the interviewer to follow your thoughts and understand your points.

Non-Verbal Communication

In online communication, non-verbal cues play a significant role. Maintain eye contact by looking directly at the camera, not the screen. Use facial expressions and hand gestures to emphasize points, but avoid excessive movements that could be distracting. Pay attention to your posture too; sit upright and lean slightly forward to show engagement and confidence.

Active Listening

Active listening is a vital part of communication. Show that you're engaged by nodding in agreement, providing feedback, and asking relevant questions. Avoid interrupting the interviewer; instead, wait for them to finish speaking before you respond.

Managing Technical Issues

Technical glitches can disrupt communication flow. If you experience any issues, calmly explain the problem and try to resolve it quickly. If necessary, suggest rescheduling or switching to a phone call.

Practice Makes Perfect

Prepare and practice common interview questions to ensure you can communicate your answers. Mock interviews with friends or mentors can provide valuable feedback and help you refine your online communication skills.

By mastering clear online communication, you'll be well-equipped to impress potential employers in any virtual interview. This skill, combined with other interview strategies, will aid you in navigating your dream job, even during a recession.

The Art of Following Up After a Virtual Interview

In the current economic climate, virtual interviews have become the norm. They offer a convenient way for employers to meet with potential candidates from anywhere in the world. But the process doesn't end when the interview concludes. The follow-up is just as crucial and requires careful thought and execution. This chapter explores the significance of following up after a virtual interview, an essential aspect of your virtual interview skills, that can help you secure your dream job during a recession.

Why Follow-Up Matters

Following up after a virtual interview shows your continued interest in the position and appreciation for the interviewer's time. It also provides an opportunity to reiterate your suitability for the role or address any points that you feel didn't come across well during the interview.

Timing Your Follow-Up

The timing of your follow-up is crucial. It's generally best to send a follow-up email within 24 hours after the interview. This timeframe allows the interviewer to still remember you clearly, while also showing your eagerness and promptness.

Crafting Your Follow-Up Message

Your follow-up message should be tailored to reflect the conversation you had during the interview. Start by thanking the interviewer for their time. Then, express your continued enthusiasm for the role and the company. If any standout moments or discussions during the interview solidified your interest in the position, mention those. This personal touch can help you stand out from other candidates.

If there are any points you didn't get to discuss during the interview or any questions that arose afterward, this is your chance to bring them up. However, keep your message concise and focused.

Handling the Waiting Period

After you've sent your follow-up message, be prepared for a potentially lengthy waiting period. Different companies have different hiring processes, and it can take a while for them to make a decision. Be patient, and avoid sending multiple follow-up messages, which can come off as desperate or pushy.

If you haven't heard back after a week or two, it's acceptable to send another follow-up message to check in on the status of your application. Keep this message polite and professional, expressing your continued interest in the role.

In today's competitive job market, particularly during a recession, every stage of the interview process is crucial. By mastering the art of follow-up, you can enhance your chances of landing your dream job.

Chapter 12: Behavioral and Technical Interviews

In today's competitive job market, it is essential to have the right skills and knowledge to stand out from other applicants. This chapter will explore the two main types of interviews – behavioral and technical – that are often used by recruiters when assessing candidates for a role. We'll look at common questions asked in each type of interview, strategies for answering them effectively, and how AI tools like ChatGPT can help you ace your next virtual interview. Finally, we'll discuss ways to prepare yourself mentally and emotionally for an upcoming interview so that you bring your best self forward during this critical moment in your career journey.

Understanding Behavioral Interview Questions

In the challenging journey of navigating your dream job, especially during a recession, understanding behavioral interview questions is an integral part. This chapter aims to provide thorough insights into behavioral interview questions and how they differ from traditional technical interviews.

What are Behavioral Interview Questions?

Behavioral interview questions are a unique set of inquiries that employers use to understand how you've acted in specific situations in the past. The main premise behind these questions is that your past behavior is a reliable indicator of how you will act in future scenarios. Unlike technical interviews that assess your skills and knowledge, behavioral interviews aim to gauge your soft skills such as problem-solving, leadership, and teamwork.

Examples of behavioral interview questions include:

1. Tell me about a time when you had to work effectively under pressure.
2. How do you handle a challenge?
3. Describe a situation where you disagreed with a team member. How did you resolve it?
4. Can you share an instance when you made a mistake? How did you handle it?
5. How do you prioritize projects under pressure?

Importance of Behavioral Interview Questions

During a recession, companies often tighten their belts and look for employees who can not only perform technically but also exhibit strong soft skills. Behavioral interview questions become more critical during this period as they help identify candidates who can adapt to changes, handle stress, and contribute positively to the company culture even in tough times.

Preparing for Behavioral Interview Questions

The best way to prepare for behavioral interview questions is by using the STAR method - Situation, Task, Action, Result.

- **Situation**: Start by describing a situation or a challenge you faced.
- **Task**: Explain the task you were responsible for in that situation.
- **Action**: Discuss the actions you took to address the situation or complete the task.
- **Result**: Finally, share the outcomes of your actions.

By structuring your responses in this manner, you can provide complete answers that give interviewers a clear picture of your capabilities.

Tips for Answering Behavioral Interview Questions

Here are a few tips to keep in mind while answering behavioral interview questions:

- Be honest: Authenticity carries weight. Share real experiences and be truthful in your responses.
- Practice: Anticipate common behavioral questions and rehearse your answers. Remember, practice makes perfect.
- Be concise: While it's important to provide context, avoid overly long responses. Aim for clarity and conciseness.

- Reflect: After explaining the situation and actions, reflect on what you learned from the experience and how it helped your growth.

Understanding and effectively responding to behavioral interview questions can make you stand out in the competitive job market, especially during a recession. As you navigate toward your dream job, remember that every question in an interview is an opportunity to demonstrate your skills, experiences, and character.

Preparing for Technical Questions

In the quest to secure your dream job during a recession, it's crucial to understand that both behavioral and technical interviews play a significant role in the hiring process. This chapter will focus on preparing for technical questions, which can be one of the most challenging aspects of the interview process.

Understanding Technical Interview Questions

Technical interview questions are designed to assess your knowledge and skills relevant to the job role. Unlike behavioral interview questions that gauge your soft skills, technical questions are more focused on your hard skills, such as programming languages for a software engineer, financial modeling for an investment banker, or digital marketing strategies for a marketing professional.

The Importance of Technical Questions during a Recession

During a recession, the job market becomes highly competitive due to layoffs and fewer job openings. Companies want to ensure they hire the best talent who can contribute immediately without requiring extensive training. Therefore, acing the technical interview becomes even more critical during these times.

Preparing for Technical Interview Questions

Here are some strategies to help you prepare for technical interview questions:

Deepen Your Understanding of the Job Role

Start by thoroughly understanding the job role and the technical skills it requires. Go through the job description in detail and note down the key technical skills required.

Brush Up on Basics

Once you've identified the key skills, make sure you have a strong foundation in these areas. Often, interviewers start with basic questions to test your fundamental understanding.

Stay Updated with Industry Trends

In technical fields, trends change rapidly. Staying updated with these changes and mentioning them during the interview can give you an edge over other candidates.

Practice Problem-Solving

Technical interviews often involve problem-solving questions. Practice such questions related to your field to improve your problem-solving skills.

Mock Interviews

Consider conducting mock interviews with a mentor or a friend. This can help you get comfortable with articulating your thought process and dealing with unexpected questions.

Tips for Answering Technical Interview Questions

While answering technical questions, keep the following tips in mind:

Explain Your Thought Process: Don't just focus on the final answer. Explain your thought process and the steps you took to arrive at the solution.

Don't Fake Knowledge: If you don't know the answer, it's okay to admit it. It's better to be honest than to provide incorrect information.

Use Relevant Examples: If possible, use examples from your past work or projects to demonstrate your technical skills.

Stay Calm and Composed: It's natural to feel nervous but try to stay calm. Remember, the goal of the technical interview is not just to test your knowledge, but also to see how you handle challenging situations.

Navigating your dream job during a recession can seem daunting, but with the right preparation and mindset, you can shine in your technical interviews and move one step closer to your dream job.

Using the STAR Method: A Tool for Navigating Behavioral and Technical Interviews

In the pursuit of your dream job during a recession, a crucial aspect to master is the art of interviews, both behavioral and technical. In this chapter, we will delve into the STAR method—an invaluable tool that can be used to effectively navigate these interviews and stand out among other candidates.

Understanding the STAR Method

The STAR method is a structured way of responding to interview questions that require you to describe a specific situation or task. The acronym stands for Situation, Task, Action, and Result. This method provides a logical and efficient framework to answer complex behavioral and even technical interview questions with real-life examples.

Situation

Begin your response by setting the scene—describe the context or background of the situation. This could be a particular project you were working on, a problem that had arisen, or an event that occurred in a previous role.

Task

Next, explain the task at hand. This refers to your responsibility in the situation. Be clear about what was expected of you and the challenges that you faced.

Action

This is where you detail the steps you took to address the task. Highlight the skills and techniques you employed, providing a detailed explanation of your actions.

Result

Finally, discuss the outcome of your actions. It's essential to focus on positive results, but it's equally important to reflect on lessons learned even if the result was not entirely successful.

Relevance of the STAR Method

During a recession, the job market becomes increasingly competitive, and employers are more selective. They seek candidates who can demonstrate resilience, adaptability, and problem-solving skills. The STAR method allows you to showcase these traits effectively by providing concrete examples from your past experiences.

Applying the STAR Method to Behavioral Interviews

Behavioral interviews focus on how you've handled various work situations in the past. Questions like "Tell me about a time when you led a team through a difficult project" or "Describe a situation where you had to make a tough decision" are perfect candidates for the STAR method. By organizing your thoughts and responses using this method, you can provide comprehensive, coherent, and concise answers.

Implementing the STAR Method in Technical Interviews

Although the STAR method is primarily used for behavioral interviews, it can also be adapted for technical interviews. For instance, you could use it to describe a situation where you used a particular technical skill to solve a problem. The 'Action' part of your response can delve into the technicalities of your approach, while the 'Result' can focus on the successful resolution of the issue.

Mastering the STAR method can give you a significant advantage in your job search during a recession. This technique offers a structured approach to answering interview questions, allowing you to highlight your skills and experiences effectively. As you navigate towards your dream job, remember that every question is an opportunity to demonstrate your abilities and potential value to the employer. With the STAR method, you can seize these opportunities with confidence.

Demonstrating Problem-Solving Skills in Behavioral and Technical Interviews

In the journey towards landing your dream job in a recession, demonstrating problem-solving skills during interviews can be a game-changer. This chapter will delve into how to effectively showcase these skills during both behavioral and technical interviews.

Understanding Problem-Solving Skills

Problem-solving skills involve the ability to handle difficult or unexpected situations and challenges at the workplace. These skills allow you to identify a problem, analyze it, and find an effective solution. Problem-solving is highly valued by employers as it is crucial for productivity and efficiency in any role.

The Importance of Problem-Solving Skills During a Recession

During a recession, companies face numerous challenges such as budget cuts, layoffs, and reduced demand. As such, they value employees who can think on their feet and solve problems effectively. Candidates who demonstrate strong problem-solving skills are likely to stand out, as they show potential to help the company navigate through tough times.

Demonstrating Problem-Solving Skills in Behavioral Interviews

Behavioral interviews are designed to assess how you've handled specific situations in the past. Interviewers often ask questions about how you've solved problems to understand your approach and thinking process.

To demonstrate your problem-solving skills in a behavioral interview, use the STAR method: Situation, Task, Action, Result. Begin by describing a situation where you faced a problem (Situation), explain your responsibility in that situation (Task), describe the actions you took to solve the problem (Action), and finally, discuss the results of your actions (Result).

Remember to choose examples that resulted in successful outcomes or where you learned something valuable. Also, focus on situations that highlight your analytical thinking, creativity, decision-making, and other key aspects of problem-solving.

Showcasing Problem-Solving Skills in Technical Interviews

Technical interviews focus on your hard skills and how you apply them to solve problems. They often include problem-solving exercises or questions related to your field.

To showcase your problem-solving skills in a technical interview, walk the interviewer through your thought process as you tackle the problem. Explain each step logically and clearly, showing how you would approach the problem, consider different solutions, and choose the most effective one. This not only demonstrates your technical knowledge but also your ability to apply it effectively to solve problems.

Demonstrating problem-solving skills during interviews can set you apart from other candidates, especially during a recession when companies face numerous challenges. By effectively showcasing these skills, you prove that you can add immediate value and help the company navigate through difficult times. As you continue your journey toward your dream job, remember that every problem you encounter is an opportunity to learn, grow, and demonstrate your resilience and adaptability.

Showcasing Teamwork and Leadership in Behavioral and Technical Interviews

When navigating towards your dream job during a recession, demonstrating teamwork and leadership skills can significantly enhance your appeal to potential employers. This chapter will explore strategies to showcase these key skills during both behavioral and technical interviews.

Understanding Teamwork and Leadership

Teamwork involves collaborating effectively with others to achieve a common goal, while leadership is the ability to guide, inspire, and influence a group toward achieving its objectives. Both are critical soft skills that employers look for, as they contribute to a positive work environment, project success, and overall company growth.

The Importance of Teamwork and Leadership During a Recession

In a recession, companies face numerous challenges, and the need for effective teamwork and leadership intensifies. Teams need to work more cohesively to navigate through uncertainties, and strong leaders are required to guide these teams, make tough decisions, and maintain morale. Therefore, demonstrating these skills can make you a valuable asset to potential employers during tough times.

Demonstrating Teamwork in Behavioral and Technical Interviews

During behavioral interviews, you might be asked questions like "Tell me about a time you had to collaborate with a difficult team member" or "Describe a project where your team had to overcome a significant hurdle". Responding to these questions using the STAR method (Situation, Task, Action, Result) can help you effectively showcase your teamwork skills.

In technical interviews, teamwork can be demonstrated by discussing projects where you collaborated with others. For instance, if you're a software developer, you could talk about working with other developers, designers, and product managers to build a software application.

Showcasing Leadership in Behavioral and Technical Interviews

Leadership skills can be highlighted in behavioral interviews through questions like "Describe a situation where you had to lead a team through a challenging period" or "Tell me about a time when you had to manage a conflict within your team". Again, using the STAR method to structure your responses can effectively demonstrate your leadership prowess.

In technical interviews, leadership can be demonstrated by discussing instances where you took the lead on a technical project or initiative, or mentored junior team members.

Showing teamwork and leadership skills in interviews is crucial, especially during a recession. By effectively demonstrating these skills, you can prove to potential employers that you have what it takes to contribute positively to their team and lead in challenging situations.

Chapter 13: Overcoming Challenges and Staying Resilient

In times of economic hardship, it can be difficult to stay motivated and maintain a positive outlook. But staying resilient and overcoming challenges is essential for job seekers who want to land their dream jobs during a recession. In this chapter, we will explore strategies for navigating the job market with confidence, such as developing a growth mindset, building professional networks and crafting an effective personal brand. We'll also discuss AI tools like ChatGPT which can give you an edge in the competitive landscape of today's job market. Finally, we'll bring together the key points from prior chapters in a concise manner, emphasizing the impact of AI and ChatGPT on job seeking strategies during a recession.

Dealing with Rejection: Overcoming Challenges and Staying Resilient

Navigating the path to your dream job during a recession is not without its fair share of bumps and pitfalls. One of the most significant challenges you may encounter is dealing with rejection. However, handling rejection with grace, learning from the experience, and maintaining resilience can be transformative in your journey. This chapter will delve into strategies for dealing with rejection and staying resilient.

Understanding Rejection

Rejection, especially in a job search, can be disheartening. It's an experience that can leave you doubting your abilities and questioning your worth. However, it's essential to understand that rejection is not a reflection of your value but merely a part of the process. Especially during a recession, when competition is high, rejection is often inevitable.

The Importance of Dealing with Rejection During a Recession

During a recession, job opportunities are scarce, and the number of applicants for each position is typically high. As such, rejections are more common. Learning to handle these rejections effectively can keep your morale high, help you maintain momentum in your job search, and ultimately bring you closer to your dream job.

Strategies for Dealing with Rejection

Reframe Your Perspective

One of the first steps to deal with rejection is to change your perspective. Instead of viewing it as a failure, see it as an opportunity for growth and learning. Every rejection brings you one step closer to a job that is a good fit for you.

Seek Feedback

If possible, ask for feedback from the interviewer or hiring manager. While it might be uncomfortable, it can provide valuable insights into areas you need to improve.

Practice Self-Care

Rejection can take a toll on your mental health. It's crucial to take care of yourself by engaging in activities you enjoy, maintaining a healthy lifestyle, and seeking support from loved ones or a counselor if needed.

Stay Resilient and Keep Going

Resilience is the key to navigating job rejections. Remember that most successful people have faced numerous rejections before achieving their goals. Keep refining your approach, expanding your skills, and persisting in your job search.

Dealing with rejection is a critical aspect of navigating your dream job during a recession. By maintaining a positive perspective, seeking feedback, practicing self-care, and staying resilient, you can turn rejection into a stepping stone toward success. Remember, each rejection is a sign that you are trying, and with each attempt, you're one step closer to landing your dream job.

Staying motivated during a long job search can be challenging, but there are several strategies that you can adopt to keep your spirits up and maintain your momentum.

Set Clear Goals: Having specific, achievable goals can give you a sense of purpose and direction. These could be as simple as sending out a certain number of applications each week or networking with a set number of people in your field.

Maintain a Routine: Treat your job search like a regular job. Dedicate specific hours of the day to job-searching activities – researching companies, tailoring applications, networking – and take regular breaks to avoid burnout.

Celebrate Small Wins: Received a positive response from a potential employer? Made a new connection on LinkedIn? Each of these small victories is a step forward in your job search journey. Celebrating them can help keep your motivation levels high.

Stay Positive: Staying positive can be tough when facing job rejections, but maintaining a positive attitude is essential. Practice mindfulness techniques, stay active, and surround yourself with positivity.

Network: Networking can open up new opportunities. Attend industry events, join online forums related to your field, and don't hesitate to reach out to professionals in your industry.

Keep Learning: Use this time to upskill. Take a course, learn a new software, or brush up on industry trends. This not only makes you a more attractive candidate but also helps you stay engaged and motivated.

Seek Support: Don't hesitate to seek support from friends, family, or a career coach. They can provide encouragement, share advice, and offer a fresh perspective on your job search strategy.

Remember, job searching can be a marathon, not a sprint. It's okay to have off days. What's important is that you don't lose sight of your goal and keep moving forward.

Balancing Job Hunting with Other Responsibilities

The journey towards securing your dream job during a recession is often filled with numerous challenges. One common hurdle is balancing the time-consuming process of job hunting with other responsibilities such as current work commitments, family obligations, or personal care. This chapter provides strategies to help you navigate this challenge while maintaining resilience.

Understanding the Challenge

Job hunting is a demanding process that requires significant time and energy. It involves researching potential employers, tailoring resumes and cover letters, preparing for interviews, networking, and more. When combined with other responsibilities, it can quickly become overwhelming.

The Importance of Balancing Job Hunting with Other Responsibilities

During a recession, the pressure to secure a new job can be intense, particularly if you are currently unemployed or facing job insecurity. However, neglecting other aspects of your life can lead to burnout, stress, and reduced productivity in your job search. Therefore, finding a balance is crucial for maintaining your wellbeing and enhancing your effectiveness in securing your dream job.

Prioritize Your Tasks

Identify what needs to be done urgently and what can wait. Prioritizing allows you to focus on tasks that are most likely to move your job search forward, such as applying for jobs that close soon or preparing for upcoming interviews.

Create a Schedule

Having a set schedule can help ensure you dedicate enough time to job hunting without neglecting your other responsibilities. Allocate specific hours for job-search activities and stick to the schedule as closely as possible.

Leverage Technology

Use job search engines and company websites to streamline your search and set up job alerts to stay informed about new opportunities. Tools like digital calendars, task management apps, and automatic reminders can also help you stay organized and manage your time effectively.

Practice Self-Care

Remember to take care of your physical and mental health. Regular exercise, a healthy diet, sufficient sleep, and relaxation techniques such as meditation or yoga can enhance your energy levels, mood, and overall productivity.

Seek Support

Don't hesitate to seek support from family, friends, or mentors. They can provide emotional support, help with tasks such as proofreading applications or practicing for interviews, and offer valuable advice.

Balancing job hunting with other responsibilities can be challenging, especially during a recession. However, by prioritizing tasks, scheduling wisely, leveraging technology, practicing self-care, and seeking support, you can manage this balance effectively. Remember, staying resilient and maintaining a positive outlook can significantly boost your chances of navigating successfully towards your dream job during a recession.

Managing stress and anxiety during a recession can be challenging, but there are several strategies you can employ:

Narrow your focus: Concentrate on what you can control, rather than worrying about larger economic issues that are out of your hands. This can help alleviate feelings of powerlessness.

Identify your financial stressors and make a plan: Understand what specifically is causing you stress - it could be job security, dwindling savings, or rising expenses. Once you've identified these, create a plan to address them. This may involve cutting back on non-essential expenses, seeking additional income sources or speaking to a financial advisor.

Stay positive: Remember that economic recessions are cyclical and are usually followed by periods of economic prosperity.

Exercise regularly: Physical activity can help reduce feelings of anxiety and improve your mood.

Follow a healthy diet: Eating a balanced diet can help keep your energy levels up and reduce feelings of stress.

Reduce caffeine intake: Caffeine can exacerbate feelings of anxiety and disrupt your sleep, which can in turn increase stress levels.

Seek professional help if needed: If your stress or anxiety becomes overwhelming, don't hesitate to reach out to a mental health professional. They can provide strategies and treatments to help you cope.

Remember, it's normal to feel stressed and anxious during uncertain times. The key is to take steps to manage these feelings and seek help when needed.

Please note that this advice is general in nature, and individual needs may vary. Always consult with a healthcare provider for personal advice.

Celebrating Small Wins

In the challenging climate of a recession, it's easy to feel overwhelmed. Job security may be shaky, budgets are often tight, and the dream job you're pursuing might feel like a distant hope. However, resilience is key in these trying times, and one strategy that can help bolster your resilience is celebrating small wins.

The Power of Small Wins

Small wins are those incremental steps towards your larger goal. They could be as simple as completing a particularly challenging task at work, getting positive feedback from a client, or even just sticking to your schedule for the day. These victories may seem trivial in the grand scheme of things, but their power lies in their cumulative effect on our motivation, confidence, and overall outlook.

Celebrating these small wins can make a significant difference in how we navigate through a recession. According to a study by Harvard Business School, tracking and acknowledging small accomplishments every day enhances motivation. It signals to our brain that we're making progress, which in turn fuels our desire to continue moving forward.

Overcoming Challenges with Small Wins

During a recession, the challenges can seem insurmountable. However, by breaking down these challenges into smaller, manageable tasks, we can create a series of small wins. Each time we conquer one of these tasks, we're not just moving closer to our ultimate goal; we're also building our resilience.

For example, if your dream job seems out of reach due to a competitive job market, start by updating your resume. This is a small, achievable task. Completing it is a small win that brings you one step closer to your goal. Celebrate this achievement, then move on to the next task - perhaps brushing up on relevant skills or reaching out to potential contacts in your desired industry.

Staying Resilient Through Celebrating Small Wins

Resilience isn't about ignoring the difficulties we face. It's about acknowledging these challenges and persisting despite them. Celebrating small wins is a way to stay resilient during a recession because it helps maintain a positive outlook, even when times are tough.

Each small victory is a reminder that progress is being made, no matter how slow it might seem. And each celebration is a moment of joy, a respite from the stress and anxiety that often accompany a recession.

Moreover, celebrating small wins fosters a growth mindset. As pointed out by Tracey Jazmin, when we're in a place of joy and positivity, we're better equipped to navigate setbacks and maintain our forward momentum.

In conclusion, celebrating small wins is more than just a feel-good activity. It's a powerful strategy for staying resilient during a recession, keeping us motivated and focused on our dream job, no matter how challenging the journey may be.

Chapter 14: Negotiating Job Offers

Negotiating a job offer can be intimidating, especially in a competitive market. However, it is an essential skill for anyone looking to maximize their earning potential and find the best fit for their career goals. In this chapter, we will explore how to prepare for negotiations, assess your options objectively, identify key areas of negotiation such as salary and benefits packages, and make sure you are getting the most out of any job offer. We'll also discuss strategies for negotiating with employers who may not be willing to budge on certain points. With these tips in hand, you'll have the confidence to confidently negotiate a job offer that meets your needs!

Evaluating a Job Offer

Navigating the job market and negotiating job offers can be particularly challenging during a recession. However, even in a tough economic climate, it's essential to thoroughly evaluate a job offer before making a decision. By carefully considering every aspect of the offer, you can negotiate effectively and get closer to landing your dream job.

Understanding the Full Picture

When evaluating a job offer, it's crucial not to focus solely on the salary. While compensation is undoubtedly important, other factors like job security, company stability, growth opportunities, work-life balance, and culture should also be taken into account.

During a recession, job security and company stability become even more critical. You can assess these aspects by researching the company's performance during the economic downturn. For instance, if the company has been able to maintain its workforce or continue growing, it could indicate that they have a resilient business model and sound management.

Salary Negotiation in a Recession

Negotiating salary during a recession can be tricky. Companies might have tighter budgets, which can limit their flexibility. However, this doesn't mean you should accept a lowball offer.

Start by researching salaries for similar roles in your industry using resources like Glassdoor or Payscale. This will give you a realistic expectation of what a fair salary should be. Be prepared to express gratitude for the offer and present your case for a higher salary based on your skills, experiences, and market research.

If the employer is unable to increase the base salary, consider negotiating other aspects of the compensation package. This could include benefits like health insurance, retirement contributions, or paid time off. You might also discuss performance bonuses or the possibility of a salary review after a certain period.

Growth Opportunities and Career Progression

In a recession, job stability might be your primary concern, but it's still important to think about your long-term career goals. Consider whether the job aligns with your career path and provides opportunities for learning and advancement.

During the interview process, ask about how the company supports employee growth and development. This could include training programs, mentorship opportunities, or clear career progression paths.

Work-Life Balance and Company Culture

Work-life balance and company culture can significantly impact job satisfaction. Even during a recession, it's important to find a job where you feel valued and comfortable.

Ask about the company's work hours, overtime expectations, and policies around flexible working arrangements. Additionally, try to get a sense of the company culture – do they encourage teamwork and innovation? Is there a high level of employee engagement and morale?

Evaluating a job offer during a recession might seem daunting, but by carefully considering all the factors and being prepared to negotiate, you can make an informed decision. Remember, landing your dream job is not just about securing employment during tough times, but about finding a role that will offer satisfaction, growth, and stability in the long run.

Understanding Your Worth: The Key to Negotiating Job Offers

Understanding your worth is a crucial aspect of job negotiation, especially during a recession. When the job market is tough, it's easy to undervalue yourself and settle for less than you deserve. However, knowing your worth and effectively communicating it to potential employers can help you secure better job offers and achieve your career goals.

The Concept of Worth in Job Negotiations

Your worth in job negotiations refers to the value that you bring to a potential employer. This value can be derived from various factors including your skills, education, experience, and the unique attributes that you bring to the table. In essence, understanding your worth involves recognizing the tangible and intangible aspects that make you a valuable asset to an organization.

In the context of a recession, understanding your worth becomes even more important. While companies may be tightening their belts, they still need talented individuals who can contribute to their goals and help them navigate challenging economic times.

Assessing Your Worth

Assessing your worth starts with a thorough self-evaluation. Review your skills, qualifications, and achievements. Consider the unique experiences or perspectives you offer. It's also beneficial to research market trends and understand the value of your role in the industry. Websites like Glassdoor and Payscale provide useful resources for understanding the average salary ranges for specific roles in various locations.

Don't forget to consider the less tangible aspects of your worth, such as leadership abilities, problem-solving skills, or adaptability. These traits are particularly valuable during a recession when companies need employees who can navigate uncertainty and drive change.

Communicating Your Worth

Once you've assessed your worth, the next step is effectively communicating it during job negotiations. Be prepared to discuss your achievements, skills, and the unique value you can bring to the company. Use concrete examples to demonstrate how you have added value in past roles and how you plan to contribute in the future.

If an initial job offer falls short of your expectations, don't hesitate to negotiate. Remember, negotiation is not just about demanding more; it's a discussion about your value. Approach the conversation confidently, armed with your research and a clear understanding of your worth.

Understanding your worth is a critical component of job negotiation, especially during a recession. By recognizing the value you bring and effectively communicating it, you can negotiate job offers that reflect your true worth. This not only helps you secure better compensation packages but also fosters a sense of self-worth and confidence that will empower you throughout your career journey.

Negotiating Salary and Benefits: Securing Your Dream Job During a Recession

In the throes of a recession, job-seekers often feel they're in a weaker position when it comes to negotiating salary and benefits. However, even during economic downturns, it's crucial to understand your worth and negotiate effectively to secure a fair compensation package.

The Art of Negotiation

Negotiating salary and benefits is a delicate art, particularly during a recession. It's essential to approach it with preparation and tact. First, you need to understand your market value. Research salaries for similar roles in your industry using resources like Glassdoor or Payscale. This will equip you with concrete data to back up your negotiation.

Secondly, be clear on what you want. While salary is important, the overall benefits package can also significantly impact your job satisfaction. Consider aspects such as health insurance, retirement contributions, flexible working hours, paid time off, or professional development opportunities.

Finally, remember negotiation is a two-way conversation. It's not about making demands, but rather finding a mutually beneficial solution. Be prepared to listen, show empathy, and be flexible in your negotiations.

Navigating Salary Negotiations

During a recession, businesses are often looking to cut costs, and this can impact salary negotiations. However, this doesn't mean you should undervalue yourself. If a potential employer cannot meet your salary expectations, consider negotiating other components of your compensation.

For example, you could negotiate for performance bonuses, which can be tied to the company's success and your individual performance. Similarly, you could discuss having a salary review in six months rather than waiting for the typical annual review. This could give you an opportunity for a pay increase once you've proven your value to the company.

Benefits Negotiation

Benefits can sometimes be overlooked during negotiation, but they form a crucial part of your compensation package. If a higher salary isn't on the table, there may be room to negotiate benefits.

Perhaps the company can offer more comprehensive health insurance, increased vacation days, or greater retirement contributions. Professional development opportunities, such as training programs or tuition reimbursement, can also be valuable, particularly during a recession when enhancing your skills can boost your career resilience.

Negotiating salary and benefits during a recession may be challenging, but it's a vital step towards securing your dream job. By understanding your worth, being prepared, and approaching the conversation with flexibility and empathy, you can successfully navigate these discussions. Remember, the goal is to find a mutually beneficial outcome that recognizes your value and meets your professional needs.

Handling Multiple Offers

In the midst of a recession, receiving multiple job offers can feel like an unexpected luxury. However, it also brings its own set of challenges. How do you choose between different opportunities? How can you negotiate effectively to ensure you're making the best decision for your career and personal growth? Here's how to navigate this complex situation.

The Advantage of Choice

Having multiple job offers puts you in a unique position of power. It not only validates your skills and experiences but also provides you with options to choose from. This can be particularly empowering during a recession, where job security is often uncertain.

However, it's important to handle this situation with care. While you might be inclined to simply choose the offer with the highest salary, it's crucial to consider other factors such as company culture, job security, growth opportunities, and work-life balance.

Evaluating Your Options

When evaluating multiple job offers, take a holistic view. Beyond just the salary, consider the entire compensation package, including benefits like health insurance, retirement plans, and paid time off.

Other important factors include the role itself, the team you'll be working with, the company's stability (especially important during a recession), and future career opportunities within the organization.

Respectful Negotiation

Negotiating multiple job offers needs to be done respectfully. Be transparent and let each employer know that you're considering another offer. Most employers will understand your need to evaluate your options, especially if they're aware that their offer is competitive.

Remember, negotiation isn't just about getting more; it's about reaching an agreement that benefits both parties. Be open about what you're looking for and listen to the employer's perspective.

Making the Decision

The final decision should align with both your short-term and long-term goals. Consider which offer will bring you closer to your dream job and think about where you see yourself growing and thriving.

During a recession, job stability becomes more important. Research the company's performance and future prospects. A company that's able to weather a recession might provide more job security.

Handling multiple job offers during a recession can be a complex process. It involves careful evaluation, respectful negotiation, and thoughtful decision-making. By taking a comprehensive approach, you can make a decision that not only meets your immediate needs but also brings you one step closer to your dream job.

Saying No Respectfully

During a recession, job seekers often find themselves in a delicate balancing act. On one hand, the challenging job market may make any job offer seem like a lifeline. On the other hand, it's essential to ensure that the job aligns with your career goals and offers fair compensation. Sometimes, this may mean having to decline a job offer. Here's how to say no respectfully during job offer negotiations.

Understanding When to Say No

The first step is recognizing when it might be appropriate to decline an offer. If the job doesn't align with your long-term career goals, the compensation is insufficient, or the company culture isn't a good fit, it might be in your best interest to say no. Making this decision requires a careful evaluation of the job offer and introspection about what you want from your career.

How to Decline a Job Offer Respectfully

Once you've decided to decline an offer, it's important to communicate this respectfully and professionally. Here are some key points to keep in mind:

Express Gratitude

Start by expressing your appreciation for the offer and the opportunity. This shows respect for the time and effort the employer has invested in the hiring process.

Be Clear and Concise

Clearly state your decision to decline the offer. It's not necessary to provide extensive details about why you're saying no, but giving a brief reason can help maintain transparency and professionalism. For example, you might explain that you've accepted another offer, the role isn't quite aligned with your career goals, or the offered salary falls short of your needs.

Keep the Door Open

Even if a job isn't right for you now, there may be potential opportunities with the same employer in the future. Be sure to express your continued interest in the company and your hope for potential future collaborations.

The Impact of Saying No

Declining a job offer can feel daunting, especially during a recession. However, it's important to remember that by saying no to a job that isn't right for you, you're freeing yourself to continue the search for your dream job.

Furthermore, saying no respectfully helps to preserve your professional relationships and reputation in the industry.

In conclusion, saying no to a job offer is a nuanced aspect of job offer negotiations. By handling the situation with grace and respect, you can ensure that you're making the best decision for your career, even amid a recession.

Chapter 15: Building Resilience and Emotional Intelligence

Navigating the job market during a recession can be intimidating and stressful. It's easy to become overwhelmed by feelings of doubt, fear, and failure. To stay competitive in this difficult landscape, it's essential to develop resilience and emotional intelligence.

Resilience is the ability to bounce back from setbacks with strength and courage. Emotional intelligence involves understanding your own emotions as well as those of others so that you can respond appropriately in challenging situations. These skills are invaluable when searching for a job or navigating other aspects of life during an economic downturn. In this chapter, we'll discuss how developing resilience and emotional intelligence will help you gain a competitive edge in today's job market.

Understanding Resilience

In today's volatile and uncertain job market, resilience has emerged as a critical skill. More than just bouncing back from setbacks, resilience involves adapting to change, learning from failures, and persistently pursuing your goals despite obstacles. This article, part of the book "Navigating Your Dream Job: Strategies for Success During a Recession," explores how building resilience and emotional intelligence can help you succeed in your job search during tough economic times.

Resilience in Job-Searching

Job searching can be stress-inducing, especially during times of economic uncertainty. When a recession hits, competition increases, opportunities become scarce, and the hiring process often takes longer. However, being resilient means finding opportunities where there seem to be none. It involves staying open to exploring alternative career paths or industries that may have more job opportunities during a recession.

Resilience is a muscle you can build, and focusing on your ability to get through challenging times will help. Building career resilience can help you weather economic highs and lows, even during a recession. You may face challenges, but you can be proactive in managing them and turning them into growth opportunities.

Building Resilience

Building resilience starts with adopting a positive mindset. Viewing setbacks as temporary and surmountable rather than permanent can drastically change how you approach your job search. It's also important to maintain a broader perspective and long-term outlook. Remember, a recession is a period of economic decline, but it's also a phase that will eventually pass.

Next, create a robust resilience playbook. This should include strategies for building and maintaining your skills, networking effectively, and staying adaptable in the face of changing job market trends. For instance, focus on improving both your hard and soft skills. From communication to time management, these skills can make you more attractive to employers, especially during a recession when companies are looking for versatile employees.

Emotional Intelligence and Resilience

Emotional intelligence plays a significant role in enhancing resilience. Being aware of, understanding, and managing your emotions can help you remain calm and composed during your job search, even in the face of rejection or other setbacks. High emotional intelligence can also improve your interpersonal skills, helping you network more effectively and navigate job interviews with more confidence and poise.

Moreover, emotional intelligence can aid in maintaining a positive attitude and reducing stress, both of which are crucial for resilience. By managing your emotions effectively, you can better cope with the ups and downs of a job search, stay motivated, and persevere until you land your dream job.

Resilience and emotional intelligence are crucial for navigating your job search during a recession. By building these skills, you can not only increase your chances of landing a job but also grow personally and professionally. Remember, every challenge presents an opportunity for growth, and a recession is no exception. With resilience and emotional intelligence, you can turn the adversity of a recession into an opportunity to progress in your career and achieve your dream job.

Developing Emotional Intelligence

In the current economic climate, where recessions can strike unexpectedly, emotional intelligence has become a vital asset. It is no longer just about technical skills and experience but also about how we manage our emotions and those of others. This article, linked to the book "Navigating Your Dream Job: Strategies for Success During a Recession," delves into the importance of developing emotional intelligence for building resilience and achieving career success during tough times.

The Role of Emotional Intelligence in Career Success

Emotional intelligence (EI) refers to the ability to understand, use, and manage your own emotions positively to relieve stress, communicate effectively, empathize with others, overcome challenges, and defuse conflict. In a job search, especially during a recession, EI can be the difference between landing your dream job or facing prolonged unemployment.

High emotional intelligence can help you navigate the often stressful and uncertain process of job hunting during a recession. It can help you maintain a positive attitude, stay motivated despite setbacks, and build strong relationships with potential employers and network contacts.

Developing Emotional Intelligence

Developing emotional intelligence involves four key domains according to Daniel Goleman: self-awareness, self-management, social awareness, and relationship management. Each of these can play a crucial role in managing any crisis, including a job search during a recession.

Self-Awareness: Recognizing your own emotions and how they affect your thoughts and behavior is a significant first step. Understanding your strengths and weaknesses can help you present yourself authentically and confidently during interviews or networking events.

Self-Management: Controlling impulsive feelings and behaviors, managing your emotions healthily, taking initiative, and following through on commitments are all part of self-management. These skills can help you stay focused and committed to your job search, even when faced with rejection or other setbacks.

Social Awareness: Being able to understand the emotions, needs, and concerns of others can help you connect with potential employers and colleagues. It can also help you navigate the hidden dynamics of the job market, such as recognizing which industries are thriving despite the recession and which ones are struggling.

Relationship Management: The ability to develop and maintain good relationships, communicate clearly, inspire and influence others, work well in a team, and manage conflict are all crucial in today's job market. These skills can help you build a robust professional network, which can open up job opportunities that may not be advertised publicly.

Emotional Intelligence and Resilience

Developing emotional intelligence is also key to building resilience, another critical skill during a recession. High EI can help you stay calm and composed under stress, bounce back from setbacks, and keep moving forward despite obstacles. The ability to manage your emotions, adapt to change, and maintain a positive outlook can make you more resilient, helping you navigate the ups and downs of a job search during a recession.

Developing emotional intelligence is a critical strategy for navigating your dream job during a recession. It can enhance your resilience, improve your job search strategies, and increase your chances of career success. By focusing on improving your EI, you can turn the adversity of a recession into an opportunity for personal growth and professional advancement.

Practicing Mindfulness and Self-Care

Practicing mindfulness and self-care during a recession can be crucial for maintaining mental health and overall well-being. Here are some insights based on various sources:

Manage Your Stress: During a recession, stress levels can soar due to financial instability and job insecurity. Mindfulness techniques such as meditation, deep breathing exercises, or Emotional Freedom Techniques (EFT) can help manage this stress effectively. These practices allow you to focus on the present moment, reducing anxiety about the future.

Healthy Eating: Consuming foods that support your immune system and energize your body can be part of self-care during tough times. A balanced diet can contribute to improved mood and energy levels, helping you tackle challenges more effectively.

Physical Activity: Regular exercise can reduce feelings of anxiety and depression, boost your mood, and improve sleep quality. It doesn't have to be strenuous; even a daily walk can have significant benefits.

Maintain Social Connections: Even if you're cutting back on expenses, try to maintain your social connections. This can be through phone calls, video chats, or safe in-person meetups. Social support can provide emotional relief and practical assistance during challenging times.

Prioritize Sleep: Quality sleep is vital for mental health and resilience. Establish a regular sleep schedule and create a restful environment to improve sleep quality.

Practice Mindfulness: Regular mindfulness practice reduces rumination, stress, and emotional reactivity while improving memory, concentration, and decision-making. This can be particularly helpful during a recession, where careful decision-making and stress management are essential (source).

Seek Professional Help If Needed: If feelings of stress, anxiety, or depression become overwhelming, don't hesitate to seek help from a mental health professional. Many offer telehealth services if in-person visits aren't possible.

Remember, self-care isn't a luxury; it's a necessity, especially during challenging times like a recession. By taking care of your physical, emotional, and mental health, you can better navigate the ups and downs of a recession.

Embracing Failure as Learning

In the context of a job search during a recession, embracing failure can indeed become a transformative learning experience.

During a recession, job markets become highly competitive with fewer opportunities available. In such scenarios, facing rejection or failing to secure a desired position is not uncommon. However, instead of viewing these setbacks as definitive failures, they can be seen as valuable learning experiences.

Embracing failure in this context means acknowledging that the path to securing a job isn't always smooth, particularly during a recession. It involves understanding that setbacks are often part of the process and can provide crucial insights. For instance, if you fail to progress past the interview stage for a role, it might highlight areas where you need to improve your interview skills or refine your approach.

Moreover, failure can teach resilience, an essential quality during a job search in a recession. Resilience is the ability to bounce back from adversity and keep going despite setbacks. By learning to cope with rejection and failure, you're building up your resilience, equipping you better for future challenges.

Failure also encourages adaptability. If one career path isn't working out, failure might be the push needed to explore new industries, roles, or skill sets. This openness to change can be especially beneficial during a recession when certain sectors may be hit hard, and opportunities may arise in unexpected places.

Thus, while failure can be disheartening, embracing it as part of your journey can lead to growth and eventual success. The key is to learn from each setback, adapt your strategy accordingly, and continue to persevere in your job search.

Cultivating a Growth Mindset

Cultivating a growth mindset during a recession can be a powerful strategy to navigate through challenging economic times. Here's some information I found on how to maintain and foster this mindset:

1. Embrace Challenges and Learn from Failures: A growth mindset involves viewing challenges as opportunities for learning rather than obstacles. This perspective can be particularly helpful during a recession when challenges are more frequent. Instead of being discouraged by setbacks, learn from them, and use these lessons to improve your strategies.

2. Stay Flexible and Adaptable: During a recession, conditions can change rapidly. Those with a growth mindset are open to change, able to adapt their plans and strategies as needed. This flexibility can open up new opportunities and help you stay ahead of the curve.

3. Seek Out Learning Opportunities: A growth mindset involves a love of learning. Even during a recession, look for opportunities to grow your skills and knowledge. This could involve taking online courses, attending webinars, or reading industry publications.

4. Maintain a Positive Attitude: Maintaining a positive attitude is key to a growth mindset. Even in tough times, try to stay optimistic and focused on your long-term goals. Remember, recessions are temporary, and with hard work and perseverance, you can navigate through them successfully.

5. Build Resilience: A growth mindset goes hand-in-hand with resilience. Building your ability to bounce back from setbacks will help you stay motivated and focused during a recession. This can involve practicing self-care, seeking support from others, and focusing on what you can control rather than what you can't.

By cultivating a growth mindset, you can turn the challenges of a recession into opportunities for personal and professional growth.

Chapter 16: Transitioning Careers

The job market is more competitive than ever, and during a recession, it can be even harder to secure the career you desire. For many people, this means transitioning from one career field to another or taking on additional skills to remain competitive. This chapter will explore strategies for navigating these difficult times with confidence by assessing your skills, developing a growth mindset, building professional networks, and crafting an effective personal brand. We'll also discuss how AI tools like ChatGPT can give you a competitive edge along with online resources for job seekers including government-sponsored websites and applications. By the end of this chapter, readers will have gained insight into how AI is impacting job-seeking strategies during recessions so they can better equip themselves for success in their chosen field.

Assessing Your Transferable Skills

In the midst of an economic downturn, many individuals find themselves considering a career transition. Whether this change is driven by job loss, lack of advancement opportunities, or a desire for something more fulfilling, it's a daunting prospect that can be made more manageable by accurately assessing and leveraging your transferable skills. This chapter aims to guide you through the process of identifying these valuable skills and applying them to your career transition, especially during a recession.

Understanding Transferable Skills

Transferable skills are abilities that can be applied across a range of different jobs and industries. They're not industry-specific; rather, they're flexible skills that can be utilized in various settings. Examples include communication, leadership, adaptability, self-management, and time management. These skills tend to remain relevant regardless of the state of the economy, making them particularly valuable during a recession.

Auditing Your Skills

The first step in leveraging your transferable skills is conducting a thorough audit. This involves taking stock of both your hard and soft skills, identifying areas for development, and recognizing which skills are transferable. Don't limit your assessment to just your professional life; consider the skills you've developed in all areas of your life.

Remember to be honest with yourself during this process. Identify any gaps in your skillset that you'd like to fill and think about how you can develop these areas. This could involve enrolling in online courses, attending relevant workshops, or seeking mentorship in your desired field.

Applying Your Skills

Once you've identified your transferable skills, it's time to apply them to your career transition. This might involve tailoring your resume and cover letter to highlight these skills or using them as talking points in interviews. It's also worth considering how these skills could apply to industries you may not have previously considered.

For example, if you've identified strong communication and adaptability skills, these could be invaluable in a customer service role. Similarly, if you've recognized a talent for leadership and self-management, these could be applied to a project management position.

Recession-Proofing Your Career

Transferable skills are key to recession-proofing your career. By developing a versatile skillset, you can increase your employability and resilience in the face of economic uncertainty.

During tough economic times, employers value adaptability and creativity. Having a broad range of transferable skills shows potential employers that you can adjust to new environments and bring fresh perspectives to their teams.

Moreover, maintaining an adaptable mindset and continuously building on your transferable skills can help safeguard your career against future recessions. Stay proactive about your personal development and keep an eye on emerging trends and skills in demand in the job market.

In conclusion, assessing your transferable skills is a crucial step in successfully transitioning careers, particularly during a recession. By understanding, auditing, and applying these skills, you can navigate your dream job and ensure your career remains resilient in the face of any economic climate.

Gaining New Qualifications

Gaining new qualifications during a recession can be an effective strategy for transitioning careers, and there are several reasons why.

Increased Employability: In times of economic downturn, the job market becomes highly competitive. Gaining new qualifications sets you apart from other candidates, making you more attractive to potential employers. It shows your commitment to personal and professional growth, even in challenging times.

Relevance: The nature of work is constantly evolving, and some skills become obsolete over time. By gaining new qualifications, you keep your skills relevant and up-to-date. This is particularly important in industries such as technology and digital marketing, where trends and practices change rapidly.

Versatility: Gaining qualifications in a variety of areas increases your versatility as a professional. This can open doors to new industries and roles that you may not have previously considered. In a recession, when job opportunities in certain sectors may be scarce, having a broad skill set can be a significant advantage.

Confidence: Acquiring new qualifications can boost your confidence, which is essential when you're transitioning careers. When you're confident in your abilities, you're more likely to perform well in interviews and take on new challenges in your career.

Future-Proofing: Gaining new qualifications can help future-proof your career. By continually learning and developing your skills, you'll be better prepared to adapt to changes in the job market. This is particularly important during a recession when the economy and job market are unpredictable.

Gaining new qualifications during a recession can enhance your employability, keep your skills relevant, increase your versatility, boost your confidence, and future-proof your career. It's a strategic move that can significantly aid in transitioning careers during tough economic times.

Networking in a New Industry

In the ever-evolving landscape of today's job market, particularly during an economic downturn, one constant remains: the power of networking. When transitioning careers and venturing into a new industry, building and maintaining professional relationships is more critical than ever. This chapter will explore the importance of networking in a new industry and provide strategies for success during a recession.

The Power of Networking

Networking is the process of interacting with others to exchange information and develop professional or social contacts. It's not just about who you know; it's about who knows you. When you're looking to break into a new industry, having a robust network can open doors to opportunities that may not be advertised publicly. This is especially crucial during a recession when job opportunities are scarce, and competition is fierce.

Navigating the Networking Landscape

Navigating the networking landscape in a new industry requires a strategic approach. Start by identifying key individuals, companies, and professional groups within your desired industry. LinkedIn can be an invaluable resource for this, providing access to a wide range of industry professionals and groups. Don't hesitate to reach out to people for informational interviews or advice – you'd be surprised how willing people are to help.

When reaching out, remember to be authentic and genuine. Networking is not just about what you can gain from the relationship, but also what you can offer. Even if you're new to an industry, your unique perspective and transferable skills could be valuable to others.

Networking During a Recession

During a recession, networking becomes even more important. Companies are more risk-averse, making them more likely to hire based on recommendations and proven connections. Therefore, having a strong network can significantly increase your chances of landing a job.

However, networking during a recession may look different. With fewer in-person events, online networking becomes crucial. Take advantage of virtual webinars, online industry events, and social media platforms to connect with professionals in your target industry.

Building Long-Term Professional Relationships

Remember, networking is a long-term investment. While it's easy to focus on immediate gains, such as job leads or referrals, the true value of networking lies in the relationships you build over time. By nurturing these relationships, you'll have a network of professionals who you can turn to for support, advice, and opportunities throughout your career.

In conclusion, networking in a new industry is a vital strategy for anyone looking to transition careers during a recession. It provides access to hidden job opportunities, valuable industry insights, and a supportive community of professionals. So start building your network today, and take a significant step towards navigating your dream job, even in challenging economic times.

Explaining Your Career Change: Navigating Transition

A career change, whether by choice or due to circumstances like a recession, is a significant turning point in one's professional journey. It can be daunting, exciting, challenging, and rewarding all at once. One crucial aspect of this transition is being able to effectively explain your career change. This chapter will delve into the significance of articulating your career shift and provide strategies for doing so with confidence and clarity.

The Importance of Explaining Your Career Change

Explaining your career change is not simply about telling others that you've switched professions. It's about communicating the rationale behind your decision, the skills you bring to your new role, and how your previous experience has equipped you to succeed in this new path. This is particularly important during a recession, when employers may be more cautious about hiring and you may face stiffer competition.

Crafting Your Career Change Narrative

The first step in explaining your career change is to craft your narrative. This involves reflecting on your motivations for the change, the skills you've acquired over time, and how these translate into your new industry or role.

Start by identifying your reasons for changing careers. These could range from seeking new challenges, aligning your career with personal interests or values, or adapting to job market changes induced by a recession.

Next, consider the skills and experiences you have gained in your previous roles. Which of these are transferable to your new career? Highlighting these skills can help potential employers see your value, even if you don't have direct experience in the field.

Finally, think about your achievements and how they have prepared you for this transition. Perhaps you've successfully navigated high-stress situations, led teams, or managed projects. These experiences can show your ability to adapt, lead, and thrive in your new field.

Communicating Your Career Change

Once you've crafted your narrative, it's time to communicate it effectively. This will come into play in various scenarios - networking events, cover letters, job interviews, and even casual conversations.

When discussing your career change, be honest, but also be positive and forward-looking. Focus on the skills and experiences you bring, rather than what you may lack in direct experience. Show enthusiasm for your new industry and express your commitment to learning and growing within it.

Moreover, be prepared to address concerns about your career change, especially during a recession. Employers may wonder about your commitment and longevity in the role. Reassure them by expressing your passion for the new field, your readiness to tackle new challenges, and your adaptability, a crucial trait during uncertain times.

In conclusion, explaining your career change is an essential part of your career transition journey. By crafting a compelling narrative and communicating it effectively, you can navigate your dream job transition confidently, even during a recession.

Embracing the Uncertainty of Change

Change is an inevitable part of life, and this is particularly when it comes to our careers. Whether driven by personal desire or external factors like a recession, career transitions can bring about feelings of uncertainty. However, embracing this uncertainty rather than resisting it can be a powerful strategy for success. In this chapter, we'll explore how to navigate the uncertainty of change during a career transition in a recession.

The Nature of Uncertainty

Uncertainty is often viewed negatively, associated with fear and anxiety about the unknown. However, uncertainty also holds the potential for positive outcomes. It's an opportunity for growth, learning, and new possibilities. Embracing uncertainty means acknowledging these potential positive outcomes and using them as motivation to move forward.

Uncertainty in Career Transitions

Career transitions inherently involve uncertainty. You might be unsure about whether you'll enjoy your new role, how long it will take to find a job in your new field, or how the shift will impact your lifestyle. These feelings can be amplified during a recession, as the overall economic instability adds another layer of uncertainty.

However, it's important to remember that everyone experiences these feelings during a career transition. You're not alone, and these feelings don't indicate that you're on the wrong path. Rather, they're a natural response to change.

Embracing Uncertainty

Embracing uncertainty involves shifting your mindset. Instead of viewing uncertainty as a barrier, consider it a stepping stone toward your dream job. Here are some strategies to embrace uncertainty:

1. Self-reflection: Use this time to reflect on what you truly want from your career. This can provide a sense of direction and purpose, helping to mitigate feelings of uncertainty.

2. Skill development: Use the transition period to develop new skills or enhance existing ones. This can boost your confidence and increase your employability, especially during a recession.

3. Networking: Building relationships with professionals in your new industry can provide support and advice, helping to reduce uncertainty.

4. Flexibility: Be open to different roles and opportunities within your new field. This flexibility can open up more possibilities and make the transition smoother.

5. Patience: A career transition takes time. Be patient with yourself and the process.

The Role of Uncertainty

During a recession, uncertainty can seem overwhelming. However, it's also a time of change and adaptation. Industries evolve, new roles emerge, and certain skills become highly valued. By embracing uncertainty, you can stay adaptable, seize new opportunities, and navigate your dream job successfully, even during a recession.

In conclusion, while career transitions during a recession can be daunting, embracing the uncertainty of change can turn this challenge into an opportunity. Through self-reflection, skill development, networking, flexibility, and patience, you can navigate your career transition confidently and effectively, setting the stage for success in your new field.

Chapter 17: Online Resources for Job Seekers

In today's job market, it is more important than ever to have access to the right resources to find success. With so much competition and a rapidly changing landscape, having the right tools can be essential for navigating this complex terrain. This chapter will explore some of the useful online resources available for job seekers, including government-sponsored websites and applications as well as AI tools such as ChatGPT. In addition, we will discuss how AI technology like ChatGPT can give job seekers an edge during a recession by quickly connecting them with relevant jobs that match their skills and interests. Finally, we'll bring together all the key points from prior chapters into one concise summary that emphasizes the impact of AI on current job-seeking strategies during these difficult times.

Job Search Websites and Platforms

Based on recent search results, there are several job search websites that are recognized as the best platforms for job hunting in 2023:

Indeed (https://www.indeed.com) is often hailed as one of the best overall job search websites due to its vast range of listings. It also provides a feature for users to upload their resumes for an instant review, helping them to refine their applications.

Monster (https://www.monster.com) is another top choice that boasts a robust search engine. With a multitude of job listings across various industries, it's a great platform for broadening your job search.

Glassdoor (https://www.glassdoor.com) offers a unique benefit: the ability to research potential employers. Alongside its job listings, you can find company reviews from employees, salary data, and more, giving you a comprehensive understanding of your potential workplace.

LinkedIn (https://www.linkedin.com) is a dual-purpose platform, providing both networking opportunities and a powerful job search tool. You can find job postings and connect directly with hiring managers, making it easier to get your foot in the door.

ZipRecruiter (https://www.ziprecruiter.com) is known for its efficient matching system, effectively pairing job seekers with relevant opportunities, making your search process more streamlined.

CareerBuilder (https://www.careerbuilder.com) has been a reliable job search resource for years, offering a massive database of jobs and career advice to help you navigate your job search.

SimplyHired (https://www.simplyhired.com) stands out for its aggregation of job listings from thousands of websites. It also offers handy tools like salary estimators and localized job information, providing additional insights into your job search.

Remember, these platforms' effectiveness can vary depending on your industry and specific needs. Therefore, I recommend using multiple resources in your job search for the best results.

Lastly, let's not forget about ChatGPT (https://openai.com/research/chatgpt). This AI model developed by OpenAI can assist in generating human-like text based on the prompts given to it. It could be a useful tool to help refine your resume or cover letter, ensuring you present yourself in the best possible light to potential employers.

In today's digital world, networking goes beyond face-to-face interactions. Online networking platforms offer job seekers numerous opportunities to connect with industry professionals, learn about job openings, and stay updated on industry trends. Here are some notable online networking platforms and strategies for job seekers:

LinkedIn (https://www.linkedin.com): Known as the professional social network, LinkedIn is a powerful tool for job seekers. Not only can you find job postings, but you can also connect directly with hiring managers and recruiters, join industry-specific groups, and engage with industry-related content.

Meetup (https://www.meetup.com/topics/networking-for-job-seekers/): Meetup hosts networking groups specifically for job seekers. These groups facilitate discussions, workshops, and events that can help you connect with other professionals in your field.

Professional Networking Sites: Apart from LinkedIn, there are other professional networking sites such as XING and Handshake that are worth exploring. They offer similar functionalities to LinkedIn, such as job postings, networking opportunities, and industry updates.

Online Networking Tips: When networking online, it's important to actively participate in discussions, share relevant content, and engage with your network regularly. This can be done by sharing, liking, or commenting on posts, which can increase your visibility and establish your presence within your professional community.

Diversify Your Network: According to a study mentioned on Time.com (https://time.com/6213412/online-job-search-networking-study/), networking with a diverse group of professionals can increase your chances of landing a job. This means connecting with people outside of your immediate circle, such as those you share a few mutual contacts with.

Social Media Job Hunting: Platforms like Facebook and Twitter are not just for socializing. Many companies post job listings on these platforms. Following companies you're interested in can keep you updated on job openings and company news.

Remember, online networking is about building relationships. So, make sure to interact genuinely and professionally, showcasing your knowledge and passion for your industry.

In the challenging landscape of a recession, job seekers must take proactive steps to distinguish themselves from the competition. One such strategy is continuous skill development. Fortunately, the digital age provides an array of online resources offering free courses to enhance your professional skills and knowledge.

Simplilearn SkillUp

(https://www.simplilearn.com/skillup-free-online-courses) stands out as a resource that offers a wide variety of free courses taught by global experts spanning numerous industries. Whether you're interested in data science or digital marketing, Simplilearn allows you to learn at a pace that suits you.

Great Learning Academy

(https://www.mygreatlearning.com/skill-development/free-courses), on the other hand, offers an extensive selection of free skill development courses. From artificial intelligence to digital marketing, these courses provide an opportunity to upskill and demonstrate your newly gained expertise to potential employers.

The **Google Digital Garage**

(https://learndigital.withgoogle.com/digitalgarage) platform provides personalized training to help you develop your career or grow your business. With the flexibility to learn digital skills at your own pace, it's an invaluable resource for those transitioning into digital roles.

Coursera (https://www.coursera.org/courses?query=free) is a renowned online learning platform that hosts a multitude of free courses offered by top universities and industry leaders. Coursera's offerings range from programming languages to business writing, and they can significantly enhance your career skills.

For those focusing on personal improvement, **Alison** (https://alison.com/courses/personal-development) provides free personal development courses. These courses can help you polish essential soft skills, such as time management and motivation, which are highly valued across all industries.

Lastly, the **HubSpot Academy** (https://academy.hubspot.com/courses) offers a wealth of free online courses in marketing, sales, and customer service. If you're looking to enter these fields or simply want to enhance your existing skills, HubSpot Academy is a resource worth exploring.

While these platforms offer courses for free, some may offer optional paid certificates upon completion. Therefore, it's advisable to check the details before starting a course. Nevertheless, the knowledge and skills you gain will undoubtedly make you a more attractive candidate in the job market, regardless of whether you opt for certification. Happy learning!

Blogs and Podcasts for Career Advice

In the challenging landscape of job seeking, especially during a recession, blogs and podcasts can serve as valuable resources for career advice. They offer insights into industry trends, provide practical tips for job hunting, and inspire with success stories.

One such resource is The Muse. This blog, accessible at https://www.themuse.com, provides advice on a range of topics including career paths, job applications, and workplace trends. Additionally, it features job listings and company profiles to give you a comprehensive understanding of the job market.

Career Contessa, available at https://www.careercontessa.com, is another noteworthy blog. It focuses on women's career development, offering advice on key areas such as job searching, making career changes, and honing professional skills.

The Glassdoor Blog, found at https://www.glassdoor.com/blog/, also offers a wealth of career advice along with insights into industry trends. Moreover, it provides the added benefit of company reviews and salary information, helping you make informed decisions about potential employers.

Turning to podcasts, Career Cloud Radio stands out as a valuable resource. Hosted by Justin Dux, it provides practical tips and tools specifically tailored for job hunting. Topics have ranged from resume writing to interviewing, providing a well-rounded perspective on the job search process.

Another inspiring podcast is The School of Greatness. It delves into what makes people successful and provides practical tips and insights on how listeners can apply these lessons to their careers. The stories and advice shared on this podcast can be highly motivating for job seekers.

Lastly, How I Built This, hosted by Guy Raz, shares stories from entrepreneurs, innovators, and business owners about their journeys to success. Listening to these stories can provide inspiration and valuable lessons that you can apply in your career.

Each of these resources offers unique insights and advice, so it's worth exploring a few different options to see which ones resonate with you the most. Remember, the best resource depends on your specific needs and career goals.

In the digital age, social media has evolved beyond a platform for personal connections and entertainment. It's now a powerful tool for job seekers, especially during a recession. This article will explore how to use social media effectively for job searching as it relates to the chapter on online resources for job seekers in the book "Navigating Your Dream Job: Strategies for Success During a Recession."

LinkedIn: The Professional Network

LinkedIn is often the first platform that comes to mind when discussing job searches. It's designed specifically for professional networking and job searching, making it an invaluable tool. Make sure your profile is up-to-date and showcases your skills, experience, and career goals. Engage with posts related to your industry and make connections with professionals in your field. LinkedIn also allows you to directly apply for job postings, making the application process seamless.

Twitter: The Information Hub

While not traditionally associated with job searching, Twitter can be a goldmine of information. Many companies post job openings on Twitter, sometimes even before they appear on job boards. Follow companies you're interested in and engage with their posts. You can also use Twitter to stay updated on industry news and trends, which can be beneficial during interviews.

Facebook: The Personal Connection

Facebook can be a surprising resource for job searching. Many local businesses post job openings on their Facebook pages. Additionally, there are numerous job search groups where members share job opportunities. Just remember to keep your profile professional, as potential employers may look at it.

Instagram: The Creative Outlet

Especially relevant for creative industries, Instagram allows you to showcase your work in a visually appealing way. If you're a designer, artist, or photographer, for example, having a well-curated Instagram portfolio can catch the eye of potential employers.

Using social media for job searching requires more than just browsing job postings. It's about building a professional online presence, networking with industry professionals, and staying updated on industry news. By leveraging these platforms effectively, you can increase your chances of landing your dream job, even during a recession. Remember to always present yourself professionally, as potential employers may view your profiles. Happy job hunting!

Chapter 18: Federal Employment Resources

The job market can be a competitive and daunting landscape, especially during a recession. To increase your chances of success in this difficult environment, it's important to take advantage of all available resources. This includes federal employment programs, which are designed to help individuals find meaningful work and gain the skills they need for their chosen career path. In this chapter, we'll look at some of the key government-sponsored websites and applications that provide support for job seekers.

Understanding Federal Employment

Federal employment offers a unique set of opportunities and challenges, and understanding the nuances can be critical to successfully navigating this career path, especially during a recession. This article aims to provide a comprehensive understanding of federal employment as it relates to the chapter on Federal Employment Resources in the book, "Navigating Your Dream Job: Strategies for Success During a Recession."

Federal employment extends beyond politicians and judges; it includes civilians working in areas such as law enforcement, public health, science, and engineering. These positions are often stable, offer excellent benefits, and provide opportunities to make a meaningful impact on society.

The hiring process for federal jobs is different from that of the private sector. It begins with understanding your eligibility for various positions. Websites like USA Jobs (https://www.usajobs.gov/) provide resources to help you determine which jobs you're eligible to apply for within the federal government.

Next is the application process. Federal jobs usually require specific types of work experience for a certain period. Therefore, it's crucial to show how your skills and experiences meet the job requirements. Many federal jobs also require a security clearance, a process that can take several months up to a year.

Compensation in federal jobs uses the General Schedule (GS) pay system, with base pay offered for most positions. Some highly competitive jobs, however, may offer more attractive compensation packages. The Office of Personnel Management (https://www.opm.gov/) provides detailed information about federal employee compensation packages.

Working in the federal sector also demands a commitment to diversity and inclusion. Federal agencies prioritize creating a workforce that reflects the diversity of the nation.

Therefore, understanding the values and mission of the specific agency you're interested in is crucial.

Lastly, remember that while it is not impossible to fire a federal employee, it is notoriously difficult. Therefore, federal jobs tend to be stable, but they also demand a high level of commitment and performance.

In conclusion, understanding federal employment involves familiarizing yourself with the hiring process, job requirements, compensation, and the values of federal agencies. With this knowledge, you can effectively use federal employment resources to navigate your way to your dream job, even during a recession.

Navigating USAJobs.gov

Navigating the job market during a recession can be a daunting task. However, one sector that often remains robust even in tough economic times is federal employment. A critical resource for those seeking federal employment is USAJobs.gov. This article will guide you through the intricacies of navigating USAJobs.gov, as it relates to the chapter on Federal Employment Resources in the book "Navigating Your Dream Job: Strategies for Success During a Recession."

USAJobs.gov serves as the official online portal for federal job listings across various agencies. It's designed to streamline the federal hiring process while providing tools and resources to support job seekers in their quest for employment.

To start your journey on USAJobs.gov, create a login.gov account. This single sign-on solution allows you to securely access multiple government websites with one account. To create an account, visit USAJobs.gov and click "Create Profile" on the front page. You'll be walked through a series of steps to create your account.

Once you've created an account, it's time to build your profile. Your profile serves as your online resume. Make sure it's complete and accurate, highlighting your skills, education, and experience that match your desired job. Remember, federal resumes are typically more detailed than private sector ones.

Next, use the search function to find jobs that match your skills and interests. You can filter your search by location, department, agency, and occupation. Once you've found a job you're interested in, review the job announcement carefully. It will provide important information about the job duties, qualifications, salary, and application process.

Applying for a job on USAJobs.gov involves completing an online application, answering a questionnaire, and submitting required documents. The questionnaire is designed to rate your experience and training relevant to the job. Ensure your responses mirror the information in your resume.

After submitting your application, you can track its status on USAJobs.gov. While the hiring process may take some time due to the comprehensive nature of federal hiring procedures, don't get discouraged.

Navigating USAJobs.gov effectively is a crucial step towards securing federal employment. By understanding how to create a profile, search and apply for jobs, and follow up on applications, you can leverage this platform to enhance your job search efforts, especially during a recession. With determination and the right resources, your dream of landing a federal job can become a reality.

Applying for Government Jobs

Applying for a government job, particularly during a recession, can be a strategic move for many job seekers. Government positions are known for their stability, competitive compensation, and robust benefits packages. However, the application process can be intricate and requires a different approach compared to the private sector. This article will offer guidance on applying for government jobs, specifically relating to the chapter on Federal Employment Resources in the book "Navigating Your Dream Job: Strategies for Success During a Recession."

The first step in applying for government jobs is to identify the type of position you're interested in. Government agencies offer a vast array of roles across various fields. From science and technology to public policy and administration, there's likely a government job that aligns with your skills and interests.

Once you've identified potential roles, the next step is to understand the application process. The official site for federal jobs is USAJOBS (https://www.usajobs.gov), which allows you to search and apply for federal government jobs for free. It's important to create a comprehensive profile on USAJOBS, as it serves as your resume when applying for jobs on the platform.

When applying for government jobs, it's crucial to remember that they require more detailed resumes than those in the private sector. A federal resume should include all relevant work experience, including volunteer work, internships, and full-time positions. Each job listed should include specifics such as hours worked per week, supervisor's contact information, and detailed descriptions of duties and accomplishments.

Job announcements on USAJOBS will often include a questionnaire to assess your qualifications for the position. It's essential to answer these questions honestly and thoroughly, as they play a significant part in the initial screening process.

After applying, you'll receive notifications about the status of your application via email. Keep in mind that the federal hiring process can be lengthy, often taking several months. Patience is key during this process.

Additionally, it's worth noting that some federal jobs require security clearance. This process involves a thorough background check and can add time to the hiring process.

In conclusion, while the process of applying for government jobs can be complex, it can lead to rewarding career opportunities, especially during challenging economic times. By understanding the nuances of the application process and utilizing federal employment resources, you can navigate your way toward landing your dream government job.

Preparing for Federal Interviews

In the quest for your dream job during a recession, securing a federal interview is a significant milestone. Federal interviews are unique and require specific preparation. This article will guide you on how to prepare for federal interviews as it relates to a chapter on Federal Employment Resources in the book "Navigating Your Dream Job: Strategies for Success During a Recession."

The first step in preparing for a federal interview is understanding the job announcement. It contains key information about the duties, responsibilities, and qualifications of the position. By analyzing the job announcement, you can identify the competencies and skills the agency is seeking.

Once you've analyzed the job announcement, create success stories that demonstrate these competencies. These stories should succinctly detail instances where you've applied these skills or competencies successfully in past experiences. It's advisable to prepare a story summary for your interview.

Researching the federal agency you're interviewing with is also crucial. Understanding the agency's mission, projects, and culture can give you an edge during the interview. It shows your interest in the agency and allows you to tailor your responses to align with their mission and values.

Another aspect of preparing for a federal interview is anticipating questions and rehearsing your answers. The STAR (Situation, Task, Action, Result) method is particularly useful for answering behavioral interview questions often used in federal interviews. Practice telling your stories using this method.

Clean up your online presence before the interview. Federal employers may check your online profiles, and having a professional online presence can enhance your chances of landing the job.

During the interview, be polite and professional throughout the duration. Show enthusiasm for the role and the agency, and remember to ask insightful questions at the end of the interview.

Post-interview, send a thank-you note to the interviewers. This simple act of politeness can leave a lasting impression and set you apart from other candidates.

In conclusion, preparing for a federal interview involves analyzing the job announcement, creating relevant success stories, researching the agency, practicing your answers, and maintaining professionalism throughout the process. With thorough preparation, you can excel in your federal interview and move one step closer to securing your dream job, even during a recession.

Benefits and Drawbacks of Federal Employment

In the realm of employment, federal jobs often stand out as a desirable choice for many job seekers. These positions offer a mix of benefits and drawbacks that can significantly influence an individual's career trajectory. This article aims to elucidate these aspects to provide a balanced view of federal employment.

Benefits of Federal Employment

Stability: Federal jobs are known for their stability. Unlike the private sector, where layoffs can be frequent, federal positions tend to be more secure. This is particularly advantageous during economic downturns, when job security becomes paramount.

Compensation Package: Federal employees typically receive competitive compensation packages. These packages often include health insurance, life insurance, long-term care insurance, flexible spending accounts, and generous leave policies. For more details on these packages, you can visit Federal Employee Compensation Package (https://www.opm.gov/policy-data-oversight/pay-leave/pay-administration/fact-sheets/federal-employee-compensation-package/).

Retirement Benefits: The Federal Employees Retirement System (FERS) provides retirement benefits to federal employees. This includes a Basic Benefit Plan, Social

Security, and the Thrift Savings Plan. You can learn more about these benefits at the Office of Personnel Management (https://www.opm.gov/retirement-services/fers-information/) website.

Drawbacks of Federal Employment

Slow Career Advancement: Career progression in the federal sector can be slower than in the private sector. Promotions and raises are generally based on a structured system rather than performance, which might limit ambitious employees.

Bureaucracy: The federal sector is known for its bureaucracy. The decision-making process can be slow and involve multiple levels of approval. This may lead to frustration, particularly for those used to a fast-paced work environment.

Limited Innovation: Due to the nature of government work, there can be less room for innovation. Strict regulations and protocols might limit creativity and entrepreneurial spirit.

In conclusion, while federal employment offers several benefits, including job security, competitive compensation, and robust retirement plans, it also has its drawbacks. The pace of career advancement, the bureaucratic nature of work, and the limited scope for innovation are potential challenges. Therefore, individuals considering federal employment should weigh these factors carefully to make an informed decision.

Chapter 19: Concluding Remarks – Making It to the Finish Line!

Navigating your dream job during a recession requires resilience and determination. You must be prepared to face the challenges of an increasingly competitive job market, while still maintaining optimism about your future career prospects. In this chapter, we will bring together the key points from prior chapters in a concise manner, emphasizing the impact of AI and ChatGPT on job-seeking strategies during a recession. We will also discuss how to assess skillset gaps, develop a growth mindset for success, build professional networks for support and guidance, craft an effective personal brand that stands out in the crowd, and find online resources for job seekers including government-sponsored websites and applications. With these strategies at hand, you can confidently take charge of your career journey!

Reflecting on Your Journey

As we conclude our journey through the book "Navigating Your Dream Job: Strategies for Success During a

Recession," it's essential to reflect upon the strides taken, lessons learned, and resilience built in the face of economic adversity. This reflection is not just an act of reminiscence, but a tool to consolidate our learnings and prepare ourselves for future challenges.

The Journey Begins with Self-Assessment

The first step in navigating your dream job during a recession is self-assessment. Knowing your financial goals, understanding your skills, and identifying your passion areas are crucial. In a period of economic downturn, it's more important than ever to pinpoint what success means to you personally and professionally.

Building Resilience Through Financial Preparedness

A key part of this journey lies in building financial resilience. This involves taking practical steps like forming a budget, limiting unnecessary spending, and investing in an emergency fund. These measures create a safety net that allows you to take calculated risks in pursuit of your dream job without the fear of financial ruin.

The Art of Mindfulness in Decision Making

Another significant aspect of this journey is learning the art of mindfulness in decision-making. This can help make sound financial decisions, even under pressure. It involves being fully present in the moment, understanding the implications of your decisions, and not getting swayed by panic or herd mentality.

Adapting to Change: The Test of Flexibility

Flexibility is a vital attribute when navigating through a recession. The economic landscape can change rapidly, and having the ability to adapt quickly can be the difference between success and failure. This flexibility may involve exploring different industries, accepting roles outside of your comfort zone, or even relocating for better opportunities.

Traveling Mindfully

Traveling during a recession may seem counterintuitive, but it can be done mindfully and economically. This could mean shorter trips, selecting cheaper destinations, or utilizing reward programs. Traveling can provide a refreshing perspective, inspire creativity, and open doors to unexpected opportunities.

The Final Stretch: Persistence & Patience

The last leg of this journey is characterized by persistence and patience. Achieving your dream job during a recession will likely require more time and effort than in a buoyant economy. But remember, perseverance pays off. Keep networking, keep learning, and most importantly, keep believing in your abilities.

In conclusion, the journey to your dream job during a recession can be fraught with challenges. However, with self-assessment, financial preparedness, mindfulness, flexibility, mindful travel, and persistence, you can navigate these choppy waters with confidence. Reflecting on your journey isn't just about celebrating the victories but also appreciating the struggles that shaped you. Here's to making it to the finish line, stronger and more resilient than ever before!

Maintaining Momentum in Your New Job: Concluding Remarks – Making It to the Finish Line!

As we reach the closing chapter of our book, "Navigating Your Dream Job: Strategies for Success During a Recession," it's crucial to focus on maintaining momentum once you've secured your new job. In this economic climate, getting a job is only half the battle. The real challenge lies in proving your value and sustaining your performance amid a recession.

Embrace the Future with Foresight

The first step to maintaining momentum in your new role is developing a forward-thinking mindset. This means sharpening your focus on customers and company goals, as they are the lifeline of any business, especially during a recession. As suggested by the Harvard Business Review (https://hbr.org/2008/09/how-to-protect-your-job-in-a-recession), without customers, no one will have a job in the future.

Prioritize Recognition and Empathy

In times of recession, it's vital to prioritize recognition and empathy. According to Bonusly (https://bonusly.com/post/retention-during-a-recession-how-to-keep-top-talent), these are key drivers to retaining top performers in a recession. Show appreciation for your colleagues' work and demonstrate understanding of the challenges they may be facing. This will not only boost morale but also foster a positive work environment.

Refocus Goals and Shift Mindset

To maintain momentum in a recession, refocusing your goals and shifting your mindset are essential. As advised by Insider Career Strategies (https://www.insidercareerstrategies.com/blog/6-strategies-to-accelerate-your-career-momentum-in-a-recession/6/2020), moving with urgency and checking your ego at the door can accelerate your career momentum. Be ready to adapt to changing circumstances, and remember, humility can go a long way in building strong professional relationships.

Foster Innovation and Growth

Despite the economic downturn, fostering innovation and growth is critical to keep momentum. Evolving as a professional and contributing to your company's growth can set you apart. As outlined by Entrepreneur (https://www.entrepreneur.com/growing-a-business/how-to-keep-pace-and-grow-your-company-during-a-recession/448633), if you're not growing, you're dying. Think ahead, innovate, and always strive to stay a step ahead of the curve.

Cultivate Strong Relationships

Finally, cultivating strong relationships is a foolproof strategy for recession-proofing your job as suggested by

Exact Staff (https://exactstaff.com/career-progressing-during-economic-downturn/). Building positive relationships with your coworkers and superiors can fortify your position within the company and open doors to new opportunities.

In conclusion, maintaining momentum in your new job during a recession requires foresight, empathy, goal refocus, innovative thinking, and relationship building. It's about proving your worth, adding value, and being an irreplaceable asset to your company. Here's to not just making it to the finish line, but doing so with flying colors!

Continuing Professional Development

As we draw the final lines in "Navigating Your Dream Job: Strategies for Success During a Recession," we reach the crucial topic of Continuing Professional Development (CPD). This concept holds a significant place in our professional journeys, more so during an economic downturn.

The Importance of Lifelong Learning

The essence of CPD is embodied in the notion of lifelong learning. This principle encourages continuous knowledge acquisition, skill enhancement, and staying abreast with the latest industry trends. In the face of a recession, when job competition heightens, having an upper hand through continual learning can be a game-changer. As emphasized by Newsweek at https://www.newsweek.com/advancing-your-career-through-education-economic-downturn-

1770970, using education as a stepping stone can be a potent strategy during economic downturns.

Investing in Your Future

Forbes, at https://www.forbes.com/sites/karadennison/2022/08/12/5 -ways-to-recession-proof-your-career-in-uncertain-times/, advises that investing in your future through continuous learning is a key approach to recession-proofing your career. This could involve pursuing further education, enrolling in online courses, or participating in webinars and workshops. Besides enhancing your skills, it also demonstrates to potential employers your dedication to personal growth and adaptability.

Building Resilience Through Development

The Business Relationship Management Institute, at https://brm.institute/professional-development- resolutions/, proposes that committing to CPD, even amidst financial downturns, can cultivate resilience. This is because CPD not only arms you with the necessary skills to navigate a recession but also fortifies mental strength by fostering a growth mindset.

Dodging The Pitfalls

The Training Journal, found at https://www.trainingjournal.com/2023/continuing- professional-development-cpd/3-pitfalls-to-avoid-during- recession/, highlights that one common mistake during a recession is to cut back on learning and development. However, this can be counterproductive as it hinders the ability of individuals and organizations to adapt to changing circumstances.

The Employer's Role

Employers have a significant role in facilitating CPD. Skillsoft, at https://www.skillsoft.com/blog/the-secret-ingredient-to-thriving-in-a-recession-employee-training, suggests that continued training enhances employee engagement and ensures your team possesses the skills required to serve customers effectively.

In conclusion, CPD is not just about personal growth; it's about survival during tough economic times. It's about making yourself indispensable and resilient, capable of weathering any storm. As we cross the finish line of this journey, remember that the real race has just begun. Keep learning, keep growing, and keep moving forward!

Building strong work relationships during a recession is vital for both personal and professional growth. Here are some strategies based on my research:

Practice Empathy: According to an article on the HR Exchange Network, empathy is crucial in all aspects of business during a recession. Understanding and acknowledging the challenges that your colleagues are facing can foster stronger relationships.

Foster a Sense of Community: An article from Achievers suggests that fostering a sense of community and belonging among employees can boost morale and engagement, leading to stronger work relationships.

Establish Strong Manager-Employee Relationships: Regular communication between managers and employees can build stronger connections. As suggested by Weekly10, weekly check-ins can be beneficial.

Build a Professional Reputation: According to a post on ThomSinger.com, building a strong professional reputation can open doors to new opportunities and help you stand out in a crowded job market, indirectly strengthening your work relationships.

Invest in Personal Relationships: According to research cited by Fortune, work friendships can be what gets you through the next recession. Building these personal connections can provide emotional support and improve collaboration.

Prioritize Psychological Safety: During times of economic uncertainty, the workplace can become a source of stress. As suggested by Eletive, building psychological safety at work can help employees feel more secure and foster stronger relationships.

Remember, strong work relationships are built on trust, respect, and mutual support, aspects that are even more critical during challenging times like a recession.

Planning for Your Future Career Growth

As we wrap up our journey through "Navigating Your Dream Job: Strategies for Success During a Recession," let's turn our attention to an essential aspect that remains crucial in any economic climate - planning for your future career growth. Even during a recession, with the right approach and strategies, you can continue to grow and thrive professionally.

The Power of Upskilling and Reskilling

In an era where the only constant is change, upskilling and reskilling have become non-negotiables for career growth. This could involve enrolling in online courses, attending industry webinars, or pursuing further studies in your field. By continually learning and updating your skills, you not only make yourself more employable but also prepare yourself for future career opportunities.

The Art of Networking

Networking, often underrated, can be one of your most potent tools during a recession. It can open doors to new opportunities, provide insights into industry trends, and offer a support system during challenging times. As suggested by Forbes, even if you're introverted or dislike networking, there are ways to build these connections that can be critical for your career growth.

Embracing Career Flexibility

Flexibility, in terms of roles, industries, and even geographical locations, can significantly enhance your job prospects during a recession. This adaptability can also expose you to new experiences and skills, paving the way for long-term career growth.

Financial Planning as a Pillar of Stability

A recession often brings financial instability, making it vital to have a robust financial plan in place. This involves forming an emergency fund, limiting unnecessary expenses, and exploring additional income streams. As highlighted by CNBC, these measures can provide a safety net during uncertain times.

Prioritizing Self-Care

Physical and mental well-being forms the foundation on which your professional success is built. Regular exercise, a balanced diet, and mindfulness practices can help manage stress and keep you focused on your career goals.

Setting Clear and Flexible Goals

Having clear and realistic career goals can serve as a guiding light during a recession. These goals should be flexible to adapt to changing circumstances but firm enough to keep you motivated and focused.

In conclusion, planning for future career growth during a recession may require some adjustments but is far from impossible. With continuous learning, networking, flexibility, financial planning, self-care, and goal setting, you can not only survive a recession but come out stronger, ready for whatever comes next. Here's to not just reaching the finish line but doing so while continually growing and evolving!

Chapter 20: Bonus Section: Freelance Bonanza!

As the job market becomes increasingly competitive, more and more people are turning to freelance work as an alternative source of income. Freelance projects can provide a great way for individuals to gain skills and experience with the potential for long-term financial stability. In this bonus section, we will explore how ChatGPT can be used to locate freelancing opportunities and how AI tools like Appen's Talent Marketplace can help you find and manage your next project. We'll also provide tips on crafting an effective personal brand that stands out from the competition, as well as strategies for networking in virtual spaces so you can build strong relationships with clients. Finally, we'll discuss government-sponsored websites and applications that offer additional resources to help freelance workers succeed in their endeavors.

Understanding Freelancing

In the ever-changing landscape of employment, freelancing has emerged as a viable and often lucrative career path. This flexible way of working becomes even more relevant during times of economic uncertainty, such as a recession. In this context, we delve into the topic of 'Understanding Freelancing' in relation to the bonus chapter 'Freelance Bonanza!' from our book, "Navigating Your Dream Job: Strategies for Success During a Recession."

The Rise of Freelancing in a Recession

Recessions generally lead to job losses and cutbacks, but they also open avenues for freelance work. According to research from the Wharton School at the University of Pennsylvania, one of the first measures companies take in a recession is to reduce their overall labor costs. This opens the door for freelancers as businesses seek cost-effective ways to complete tasks without the commitment of full-time employees.

Freelancing: A Strategic Approach

Freelancing during a recession can be more than just a stop-gap measure. It can be a strategic approach to secure income and develop professionally. By offering services that are in demand during a downturn, freelancers can carve out their niche. For instance, digital skills like online marketing and virtual assistance can be particularly valuable during times when businesses are striving to maintain their online presence and efficiency.

Making Your Freelance Business Recession-Proof

While the prospect of increased opportunities is encouraging, it's essential to make your freelance business recession-proof. This includes strategies like signing

243

retainers with clients to ensure a steady stream of work, limiting expenses to manage your cash flow better, taking deposits for large projects to guard against non-payment, and diversifying your client base to spread risk.

Thriving as a Freelancer During a Recession

Freelancing during a recession isn't without its challenges, but with the right strategies, you can not only survive but thrive. Positioning yourself strategically in the market, keeping tabs on industry trends, and continuously developing your skills can help you stay ahead of the game.

In conclusion, while a recession may seem like a daunting time to pursue your dream job, it can be a bonanza for freelancers willing to adapt and seize the opportunities it presents. By understanding the dynamics of freelancing during a recession and applying the strategies discussed, you can navigate your way to success even in challenging economic times.

Finding Freelance Work

In the world of work, freelancing has emerged as a robust and flexible career path. This becomes especially significant during economic downturns like recessions. In this article, we explore the concept of 'Finding Freelance Work' as it relates to the bonus chapter 'Freelance Bonanza!' in our book, "Navigating Your Dream Job: Strategies for Success During a Recession."

The Opportunity of Freelancing in a Recession

A recession, although challenging, can create unexpected opportunities for freelancers. Companies looking to cut costs often turn to freelancers to fulfill their needs without the commitment of full-time employment. As a result, the demand for freelance work can increase during a recession, turning it into a bonanza for those ready to seize the opportunity.

Developing Relevant Skills for Freelance Work

The key to finding freelance work during a recession is to offer skills that are in high demand. In an economic downturn, businesses often prioritize services that help them stay afloat and remain competitive. Digital skills, such as online marketing, virtual assistance, graphic design, and programming, become particularly valuable. By upskilling or reskilling in these areas, you can increase your chances of finding freelance work.

Making Your Freelance Business Recession-Proof

To ensure a steady stream of freelance work during a recession, it's crucial to make your business recession-proof. This involves several strategies, including signing retainer agreements with clients, reducing non-essential expenses, taking deposits for large projects, and diversifying your client base. These tactics can help you maintain a stable income even when the economy is struggling.

Positioning Yourself for Freelance Success

Finding freelance work in a recession also requires strategic self-promotion. You need to communicate the value you offer to potential clients effectively. Highlight how your services can help businesses cut costs, improve efficiency, or overcome the challenges of a recession. By positioning yourself as a valuable partner rather than just a service provider, you can increase your appeal to prospective clients.

In conclusion, a recession might seem like a daunting time to pursue freelance work, but it can be a bonanza for those willing to adapt and seize the opportunities it presents. By understanding the dynamics of freelancing during a recession, developing in-demand skills, making your business recession-proof, and positioning yourself strategically, you can navigate your way to success in the freelance marketplace, even in challenging economic times.

Setting Your Rates

In the world of freelancing, one of the most critical decisions you'll make is setting your rates. This decision not only affects your income but also how potential clients perceive the value of your services. In this section, we will explore 'Setting Your Rates' about the bonus chapter 'Freelance Bonanza!' from our book, "Navigating Your Dream Job: Strategies for Success During a Recession."

The Art and Science of Setting Freelance Rates

Setting freelance rates is both an art and a science. It involves understanding market rates for your services, factoring in your experience and skill level, and considering your own financial needs. However, during a recession, the dynamics can change. Companies may be working with tighter budgets, and there may be increased competition from other freelancers. Despite these challenges, it's crucial not to undervalue your work.

Maintaining Your Rates During a Recession

A common misconception is that freelancers should lower their rates during a recession to attract more clients. While it's important to be flexible and understanding of clients' financial constraints, it's equally important to maintain the value of your work. Rather than lowering your rates, consider offering different pricing models or packaging your services differently to provide more value to your clients.

Communicating the Value of Your Services

Part of setting your rates is effectively communicating the value you bring to your clients. This becomes even more critical during a recession when businesses are looking for cost-effective solutions. Highlight how your services can help businesses navigate the challenges of a recession, whether by improving efficiency, reducing costs, or providing essential skills they may not have in-house.

247

Diversifying Your Client Base

One of the best ways to maintain your rates during a recession is to diversify your client base. By working with clients across different industries, you can mitigate the risk of losing income if one industry is hit hard by the recession. This approach can also open up new work opportunities, enabling you to maintain—or even increase—your rates.

In conclusion, setting your rates as a freelancer during a recession doesn't necessarily mean lowering them. By understanding your value, communicating it effectively to clients, and diversifying your client base, you can navigate the challenges of a recession and turn it into a freelance bonanza. Remember, the key to success in freelancing— during both boom times and recessions—is adaptability. The more you can adapt to changing market conditions, the more successful you'll be.

Managing Your Time and Projects

In the realm of freelancing, effective time and project management are crucial to success. In this context, we delve into 'Managing Your Time and Projects' in relation to the bonus chapter 'Freelance Bonanza!' from our book, "Navigating Your Dream Job: Strategies for Success During a Recession."

The Importance of Time and Project Management in Freelancing

As a freelancer, you're your own boss. This means having the freedom to set your schedule and choose your projects, but it also means being solely responsible for managing your time and workload. During a recession, these skills become even more critical as you may need to juggle multiple projects or clients to maintain a steady income.

Effective Time Management Strategies

Effective time management is key to maximizing productivity and maintaining work-life balance, both of which can be challenging during a recession. One strategy is to prioritize tasks based on their urgency and importance. Another is to break larger tasks into smaller, manageable parts. Using digital tools like calendars, task management apps, and timers can also help keep you on track.

Successful Project Management in a Recession

Project management involves planning, organizing, and overseeing tasks to successfully complete a project. During a recession, clients may have tighter budgets and higher expectations, putting more pressure on you to deliver high-quality work efficiently. To manage this, it's important to set clear project objectives, maintain open communication with clients, and monitor your progress regularly.

Diversifying Projects for Stability

A freelance bonanza during a recession often means diversifying your projects. Working with clients from different industries or offering varied services can help ensure a steady flow of work even if one client or industry is struggling.

Adapting to New Ways of Working

A recession can also bring new ways of working, such as remote work or flexible hours. Adapting to these changes can help you stay competitive and meet the evolving needs of your clients.

In conclusion, managing your time and projects effectively is key to navigating the freelance bonanza during a recession. By honing these skills, you can make the most of the opportunities that come your way, ensuring you not only survive but thrive in challenging economic times.

Building Client Relationships

In the world of freelancing, building strong client relationships is paramount. This becomes particularly significant during economic downturns, such as a recession.

The Importance of Client Relationships in Freelancing

A solid client relationship forms the backbone of successful freelancing. During a recession, these relationships can make the difference between a steady stream of work and an uncertain future. Clients who trust and value your work are more likely to keep you on board, even when budgets are tight.

Building Trust with Your Clients

The first step in building a strong client relationship is establishing trust. This involves delivering high-quality work, meeting deadlines, and communicating effectively. In a recession, businesses need reliable freelancers who can deliver results and help them navigate through challenging times.

Communicating Effectively

Effective communication is key to building and maintaining strong client relationships. This includes setting clear expectations, providing regular updates, and being responsive to client queries. In a recession, transparent communication about pricing, project timelines, and potential challenges can go a long way in building client trust.

Demonstrating Your Value

During a recession, it's crucial to demonstrate the value you bring to your clients. This could involve highlighting how your services can help businesses cut costs, improve efficiency, or adapt to new market realities. By showing your clients that you're not just a service provider but a valuable partner, you can strengthen your relationship and secure ongoing work.

251

Nurturing Long-term Relationships

Building client relationships isn't a one-time effort but an ongoing process. Regular check-ins, offering insights, and going the extra mile can help transform a one-off project into a long-term collaboration. During a recession, these long-term client relationships can provide stability and open up new opportunities.

In conclusion, building strong client relationships is key to navigating the freelance bonanza during a recession. By establishing trust, communicating effectively, demonstrating your value, and nurturing long-term relationships, you can secure ongoing work and maintain a stable freelance career, even in challenging economic times.

Bonus Links

Here are some valuable links to pursue your freelancing opportunities!

1. **Upwork** - A platform for freelancers in various fields. www.upwork.com
2. **Fiverr** - A marketplace for creative & digital services. www.fiverr.com
3. **Freelancer** - A large outsourcing marketplace. www.freelancer.com
4. **Toptal** - A freelance jobs site for top 3% freelancers. www.toptal.com
5. **Guru** - A platform that allows freelance workers to showcase their skills and services. www.guru.com
6. **Behance** - A platform for creative professionals to showcase their work. www.behance.net
7. **PeoplePerHour** - Freelance marketplace for all sorts of skills. www.peopleperhour.com
8. **99designs** - A freelance platform for designers. www.99designs.com
9. **TaskRabbit** - A platform to find local jobs in your area. www.taskrabbit.com

10. **FlexJobs** - A job board dedicated to remote, part-time, freelance, and flexible jobs. www.flexjobs.com

11. **Envato Studio** - A freelance marketplace for designers, developers, and creatives. studio.envato.com

12. **DesignCrowd** - A platform where businesses can find freelance designers. www.designcrowd.com

13. **Skyword** - Connects freelance writers, videographers, graphic designers, and photographers with brands. www.skyword.com

14. **Dribbble** - A self-promotion and networking site for digital designers and creatives. www.dribbble.com

15. **Aquent** - Provides creative staffing services for freelancers. www.aquent.com

16. **Craigslist** - An American classified advertisements website with sections devoted to jobs. www.craigslist.org

17. **SimplyHired** - A job search engine. www.simplyhired.com

18. **Smashing Jobs** - Job board from Smashing Magazine for designers and developers. www.smashingmagazine.com/jobs

19. **Gigster** - A platform for hiring tech freelancers like developers and designers. www.gigster.com

20. **AngelList** - A website for startups, angel investors, and job-seekers. www.angel.co

21. **Linkedin ProFinder** - Professional services marketplace that helps to connect freelancers with businesses. www.linkedin.com/profinder

22. **Dice** - A job search engine for technology professionals. www.dice.com

23. **Etsy** - An e-commerce website focused on handmade or vintage items and craft supplies. www.etsy.com

24. **Voice123** - A marketplace for voice over talent. www.voice123.com

25. **Clickworker** - A micro job site that pays for small tasks like text creation and data categorization. www.clickworker.com

26. **Rover** - A dog-sitting platform where you can apply to become a sitter. www.rover.com

27. **Teachable** - Allows you to create and sell online courses. www.teachable.com

28. **Tutor.com** - An online tutoring company. www.tutor.com

29. **Chegg Tutors** - An online tutoring site. www.chegg.com/tutors

30. **Codementor** - A marketplace for software developers. www.codementor.io

31. **Writing Jobz** - Provides writing jobs for freelancers. www.writingjobz.com

32. **iFreelance** - A platform for freelancers in all industries. www.ifreelance.com

33. **Photography Jobs Online** - A platform for freelance photographers. www.photography-jobs.net

34. **Programmer Meet Designer** - A site for programmers, web developers and designers to meet. www.programmermeetdesigner.com

35. **Rent a Coder** - A site to find coding jobs. www.rentacoder.com

36. **Zirtual** - A platform for hiring virtual assistants. www.zirtual.com

37. **Art Wanted** - A platform for artists to share, sell and offer their work. www.artwanted.com

38. **Jingle Punks** - A platform for musicians to sell their music. www.jinglepunks.com

39. **Project4Hire** - A platform for freelancers to find work in a wide range of areas. www.project4hire.com

40. **CrowdSPRING** - A platform for creatives in graphic design, industrial design, and writing. www.crowdspring.com

41. **WorkMarket** - An ADP company that helps businesses and skilled professionals connect. www.workmarket.com

42. **TranslatorsCafe** - A platform for translators. www.translatorscafe.com

43. **Daylancer** - A freelance job board. www.daylancer.com

44. **Freelance Writing Gigs** - A community for freelance writers. www.freelancewritinggigs.com

45. **Spare5** - A site that pays for small tasks. www.app.spare5.com

46. **YourMechanic** - A platform for car mechanics to find jobs. www.yourmechanic.com

47. **Field Engineer** - A platform for engineers and IT professionals. www.fieldengineer.com

48. **ServiceScape** - A marketplace for professionals in editing, translation, graphic design, and writing. www.servicescape.com

49. **LocalSolo** - A freelance job board for many cities around the world. www.localsolo.com

50. **Handy** - A platform for handyman services. www.handy.com

This list includes platforms for various professions and areas of expertise. Please remember to always do your own research and verify the legitimacy of any site before signing up and providing personal information.

Final Thoughts

Navigating the job market during a recession can be challenging, but it doesn't have to be overwhelming. With the right strategies and tools in hand, you can make the most of this difficult situation and secure your dream job or freelance career. By assessing your skills, developing a growth mindset, building professional networks and crafting an effective personal brand combined with leveraging AI-powered tools like ChatGPT for competitive edge will give you an advantage over other applicants. The key is to stay flexible and adaptive so that you are able to take full advantage of any opportunities that come your way. We hope that our book has helped equip you with all the necessary knowledge on how to navigate successfully through this ever-changing landscape! Good luck!

Meet the Author

Meet Dr. Gary Covella, a passionate seeker of business mysteries and a zestful embracer of life. Armed with a Ph.D. in Business Administration and Organizational Development, he transcends the realm of ordinary researchers by weaving captivating stories that bring complex concepts to life. When not engrossed in his work or making a positive impact on others' lives, Dr. Covella takes to the skies, finding solace and freedom as an avid aviator. Residing on Florida's enchanting Gulf Coast with his beloved spouse, he cherishes every ground-level and soaring moment, embodying a spirit of adventure that knows no bounds.